I0092288

Shona Sentential Names:
A Brief Overview

Jacob Mapara

Langaa Research & Publishing CIG
Mankon, Bamenda

Publisher

Langaa RPCIG
Langaa Research & Publishing Common Initiative Group
P.O. Box 902 Mankon
Bamenda
North West Region
Cameroon
Langaagrp@gmail.com
www.langaa-rpcig.net

Distributed in and outside N. America by African Books Collective
orders@africanbookscollective.com
www.africanbookcollective.com

ISBN:9956-790-75-3

© Jacob Mapara 2013

DISCLAIMER
All views expressed in this publication are those of the author and do
not necessarily reflect the views of Langaa RPCIG.

Table of Contents

Preface...v

Acknowledgements...................................... ix

Chapter I: Introduction.............................. 1

Chapter II: Shona Names as Heritage and Cultural Expressions... 33

Chapter III: The Socio-cultural Names of the Manyika... 53

Chapter IV: Some Shona Theophoric Sentential Names... 89

Chapter V: *Chimurenga* Names...................... 111

Chapter VI: Conclusion.............................. 149

References..155

Table of Contents

Chapter I: ...

Chapter II: ...

Chapter III: ...

Chapter IV: ...

Preface

This book is about names, and not just any names, but human names or anthroponyms as well as how they are used by the Manyika of eastern Zimbabwe. The Manyika are found in both Mutasa and Nyanga districts of Manicaland. It is again not just about Manyika names, but how the Manyika have used a special category of names to convey their feelings, thoughts as well as belief systems. The book specifically focuses on sentential names and how the Manyika, like other Shona groups have used them to respond to their immediate environment, both social and political.

This book grew out of the desire by the researcher to fill a gap that he saw as yawning in as far as research on the Manyika, especially in the area of language is concerned, and more, so in the area of onomastics where as far as the researcher is concerned very little has been done, the exception being Mapara, Nyota and Mutasa's 2011 Shona Names as Communication and Description: A case of the Manyika, which is a publication on Manyika names. The focus of these three however was general in that they focused on both anthroponyms and toponyms. The book is as well a product of the realisation that since Fortune in the 1950s, there has been little active research in the area of linguistics in this Province.

While it is true that the researcher focuses on the Manyika in his book, the other purpose of this study is to contribute to the body of knowledge that exists in Zimbabwe on names. The other studies like Pongweni's What's in a Name? (1983) focus mostly on all types of names, yet this study has only zeroed in on names that are complete statements, and are therefore full communicative tools.

This book is also as much of an anthropological one as it is linguistic. It will help readers to understand that among the Manyika, just like among the other Shona, and the other Bantu language groups at large, names do play a very significant communicative role in people's lives. They function as a window through which outsiders can look through and hopefully have a better understanding of the Manyika in particular and the Shona in general. The very same names as well function as a podium on which the Manyika strut and showcase their heritage to the world at large.

The other readers who are targeted by the book besides college and university students in various humanities and social sciences areas are academics and other interested parties in language and cultural industries. The other parties who will reap positive rewards from this book are linguists, sociologists, historians as well as some religious leaders from different religious backgrounds and persuasions. Linguists, especially sociolinguists and those in the field of pragmatics will benefit immensely given the fact that these names are speech events and acts, each in itself, and they need to be further unpacked linguistically.

Since all these names are about social relations, and how people respond to the social environment, the sociologists and anthropologists also stand to benefit. Those in the field of history, especially those who are interested in resistance movements in Europe during the Second World War and liberation war movements in Africa, Asia and Latin America will as well learn something that may inform them on the activities as well as the names that the guerrillas in these different war arenas bore, and why. The names are also of great significance to those in the area of Religious Studies, not only with regards to the Christian religion, but also to other religions where there is need to find out how religious names have fared and have been deployed as confessions and conveyors of faith.

Jacob Mapara
Masvingo, Zimbabwe
April 2013

Acknowledgements

I would like to thank everyone who participated in one way or another in assisting me to shape and reshape this book. Without insights of these colleagues who are too numerous to mention, this work would not have seen the light of day.

There are however people who deserve special mention – my maternal uncle Antony 'Dickson' Guta for encouraging me to keep on working hard, and my late paternal aunt Mai Matendawafa for continuously hammering into me that books and writing are the best remedy for short-circuited tempers. I would also like to acknowledge the encouragement I got from Professor Herbert Chimhundu and Dr Rabson Wuriga. Each of these two gentlemen has continued to encourage me to reach to dizzier academic heights. To all of you I say:

NDINOTENDA, NGIYABONGA, THANK YOU!

Chapter I

Introduction

Preamble

Names are words or sets of words by which a person, animal, place, or thing is known, addressed, or referred to. They are identity tags or badges of the named and the identified. They are given with the intention of relaying certain images or perceptions and they may succeed or fail in doing this. Names may carry or carry no meanings. Among the Shona of Zimbabwe as among most people of Africa, names are not just apportioned. They are given after serious thought even if they are being given to animals, things or places as well as of late after the advent of the cash economy, businesses. To name among the Shona at times amounts to making statements that may be declarations or expressions of certain ideas or thoughts. While there are many types of names that the Shona give, this study focuses on names or anthroponyms that are given to people either immediately after birth or as rites of passage.

To name also means to control and have power over someone or something. Usually one cannot name that which s/he cannot control. There are however other circumstances that see people naming particular persons, giving them nicknames not because they have power or influence over them but because they have to capture in summary form the way they relate to the named person. They may for example, as in colonial Rhodesia give a name such as *Mukandabhutsu* ([One who does not hesitate to kick/ One who is quick to kick, but actually meaning one who has a lave driver's mentality]) to a farmer or white employer who would easily kick a black person for alleged laziness or slowness at work. In that case, naming becomes an exercise of exorcising one's demons, or becomes a means of living at peace with them. The names that are also focused on in this study are significant in that although they are each a single word, they are outstanding because each one of them on its own forms a complete statement either as a real statement or as a question.

Background to the study

The study came about as a result of the realization that there is a lot of cultural history and memory that is carried in most of the names that those who are named in Shona carry. The researcher noted that among the Shona, specifically the Manyika names carry the aspirations as well as the fears of those who name. Those who name, the study noted may be parents, relatives or other close people like neighbours. There are also instances where those who name may be religious leaders who may see it fit to give names to the newly born that they consider to be 'Christian' and religious. The reference to 'Christian' is deliberate because the western variety of Christianity is one that has had a greater presence in Zimbabwe, when compared to other non-indigenous religions like Islam. This does however not mean that the other religions have not had an impact on naming practices in Zimbabwe. It is only that 'Christian names' are more present than those of any other at the moment. In some instances, people rename themselves as means of redefining themselves or asserting their presence. This reality is made in the last observation that led to the carrying out of this study was that during Zimbabwe's war of liberation, most aspiring guerrilla forces as well as those who had already under gone military training and had been deployed to the war front assumed new names. These names were in most cases names that they gave themselves not only as a cover from possible identification by the Rhodesian forces, but also as ideological names that were meant to inspire them in their fight against Rhodesian settler rule and oppression. There are however, some guerrillas who received these names from those who had recruited them or had trained them. A good example is that of Josiah Tungamirai, who got the first name of his war name from Josiah Tongogara (Makari 2003: 1). While some of the observations made in this discussion of the background to the study, what bis significant about this study is that it discusses the names identified not as a mixed bag, but as a special category of names – names that make statements or names that are sentences. This area is one that has not been delved into by those who pioneered writings on Shona names.

Defining Shona naming patterns

There is a generally held belief among the Shona that those named or identified by certain names are likely to behave in the manner reflected in the names that they carry. If one is for example, is named *Nhamo* (Suffering of all sorts), then it is generally accepted that the one so named is likely to live a life that is full of misery and suffering. Materially it is believed that such a person will not prosper, but will languish in depravity for the rest of his life. Even in marriage, there are fears that such a person may for example, have problems with his wife or children. If on the other hand one is give a name such as *Anotidaishe* (The Lord loves and cares for us), it is equally believed that the Lord (read Christian God) will shower that person and his or her family with blessings. While some people continue to name their children after departed relatives, there is a growing number especially among some Christian sectors, especially denominational and apostolic ones, and strongly so, that a child should not be named after a deceased relative, be it aunt, uncle or any one of the parents, whether living or departed. The belief is anchored in the fear that if the child is named after such a person and that person had traits that the family considered to be negative; the departed's spirit is likely to influence the behaviour of the one who becomes the namesake of the long departed relative. What buttresses this fear is what is preached in most Christian churches in Zimbabwe, especially the Pentecostal ones that this amounts to worshipping one's ancestors as well as backtracking in one's faith. This researcher observed that among some apostolic sects, some religious leaders openly taught their followers to pray *"Mweya yemadzinza musanditevere"* (Spirits of the family lineage do not come after me). These words clearly highlight how much most of the followers fear having as well as giving their children names of past and late relatives. What these denominations fail to realize is that the same saintly names that they recommend such as Solomon and David or of other beatified church fathers are but names of departed fellow human beings and some of them have not had glorious lives. There is nothing saintly about them. In some instances, even non-Christians give their children names that they do not know their meanings, but are names of film or literature characters. It is interesting to note that some may fear giving their children Shona names of departed relatives because they

4

fear some form of spiritual contamination and ironically go on to give their children names such as Cleopatra whom Scullard (1970: 144) describes as one who was charming but not beautiful, energetic and ambitious that she even managed to weave her way into Caesar's heart when the latter was in Egypt and she was also later to become Antony's mistress. She did all this in an effort to regain her ascendancy to the Egyptian throne after Caesar's death (Scullard: 1970: 171). This name therefore is of one who is fickle and does not value even the bond of blood relationships. Some carry names like Bismarck yet this is the man who when he was Chancellor of Germany, hosted and presided over the imperial Berlin Conference that lasted from 15 November 1885 to 6 February 1885 that parcelled out Africa between European powers that were looking for a place in the sun.

Area of Research

The research was carried out in Zimbabwe, specifically in Nyanga district, Manicaland Province to the East of the country, and to a lesser extent, in Mutasa district also in Manicaland. The reason for choosing Nyanga was deliberate. In terms of studies of a linguistic nature, very little has been done in the area. It is only Fortune (2004) who has studied the sub-dialects of Nyanga. Other than that, very little has been done that focuses on the area. Nyanga is also one of the eastern border areas that bore the brunt of Zimbabwe's war of liberation. This is the area where the guerrillas interacted with the Carmelite Order of the Roman Catholic Church where the late Irish clergyman Donal Lamont was Bishop of the Umtali (now Mutare) Diocese. Nyanga district falls within this Church Diocese. As the guerrillas interacted with the masses, they also interacted with the church. What is however of significance about this area is that as the guerrillas interacted with the masses and the Church, they were using *noms de guerre* (what they themselves called *Chimurenga* names). Some of these names qualify to be statements, and it is a few of these names that have been selected that are also part of this study.

Nyanga as a district has also been a highly contested area on the religious front. To the north of the district are found two mission stations. There is Avila Mission that was set up by the Roman Catholics just east of Gohoto village and north of Kadyamusuma village. To the south of Bande service centre there is Elim Mission of the Elim Pentecostal Church. This denomination runs a hospital, a primary school and a secondary school. In Nyamaropa and Nyakomba there was also a contest between the Roman Catholics at Regina Coeli and the Anglicans at St. Luke's Nyakomba. The Catholics and Anglicans are also dominant at Nyatate as well as in Nyanga town. The United Methodists had also recently moved into the recently established Nyamaropa Irrigation Scheme. Nyanga is also home to the Tangwena people, who together with their Chief, Rekayi Magodo Tangwena resisted white settlerism by refusing to move away from their ancestral lands and be resettled in either Gokwe (Midlands Provivnce) or Mhandamabwe (Masvingo Province, then Victoria).Close to the Tangwena people is Mutasa District which during the war was host to some of Tangwena's people who did not move into Mozambique but opted to stay on in the country. These people, who were based at Mashena (Machena) that the Rhodesian settler regime called Holdenby were finally evicted and herded into what the Smith regime called Protected Villages (PVs) in March and April of 1977. The district is

6

significant because the Tangwena people are among those who gave their children sentential names. Some of the guerrilla names of those who operated in the Honde Valley area of Mutasa district in Manicaland Province are also the subject of the discussion of this research because they in some instances also operated in the areas like Nyamaropa and Nyadowa, two places under Chief Saunyama that played host to most of the guerrillas, some of whom bore the sentential names that are discussed in the fifth chapter of this book. It is in this boiling cauldron that different names reflecting differing and conflicting ideologies and faiths emerged. It is the existence of these names that inspired this researcher to look into sentential names which appear to have been informed by these differing situations that fortunately or unfortunately found themselves sharing the same physical, religious, political and social space.

The Manyika

The term Manyika is used to refer to speakers of related sub-dialects who are found in Manicaland Province in eastern Zimbabwe. The term 'Manicaland' is an Anglicisation of the term 'Manyikaland' which is a practice that is borrowed from the British system of naming where places where people are largely domiciled are given names that reflect this demographic dominance. A good example is the name England itself. It means place of the English. Manicaland means place of the Manyika. The Manyika are found in largely four districts of the Province's seven districts. It is also because demographically they are more than the other groups, the Hwesa and Barwe in Nyanga and the Ndau in Chimanimani and Chipinge that the Province got named after them. The sub-dialects that they speak are Guta (spoken around Watsomba in Mutasa district), Karombe (spoken around Juliasdale, Nyanga district, although all the people were moved to either near Bonda, Sedze or Nyamaropa and Katerere in Nyanga North by the Rhodesian settler regime), Unyama (also spoken in Nyanga under Chief Saunyama's area), Nyamhuka (around Triashill, Mutasa district) and Teve (also known as Bvumba spoken around Vumba, in Mutare district). The others are Bunji (spoken around Troutbeck and Matema area, Nyanga district), Nyatoro (Troutbeck, Matema and Bende) as well as Nyatwe that is spoken in the Nyatwe area that borders Triashill (Fortune 2004: 129). There are also Bocha and Jindwi that are both spoken in Mutare district as well as Ungwe that is spoken in Makoni district. For purposes of this study, the researcher only focuses on two districts, Nyanga and Mutasa. He sees them as adequate enough to represent the other Manyika. The other reason is that these districts were among the first ones that guerrillas coming into Zimbabwe would pass through on their way to the front that was constantly shifting westwards as the guerrilla war intensified.

Significance of the study

The researcher found it necessary to carry out this research after having observed that some people give their children names that have no cultural, social, religious or political significance to their being. In fact, what the researcher observed was the general misconception among some Shona speakers that some names carry with them demonic baggage that cannot be put down because it eats even into one's plans and future. They believe that one ceases to live his or her life but that of the one they are named after. The research was also found to be necessary because some people say to give children names such as *Chamunorwachiipasipanodya* (Why do you fight one another when at the end we all die) is *kumuremedza mwana* (to give the child a heavy burden) without trying to find out why people end up giving their children such names. It is important to also point out here that while this study is ethnographic as some people may observe, it is also linguistic because the study of names falls under language study and has the nomenclature *onomastics*, which means the science of the study of names.

Theoretical framework

This study is informed by several theories that relate to names. Some of these theories are: the descriptive theory, syntactic theory, semantic or Milianism theory, sense theories as well as the causal-historical theory of reference. All these theories do not agree but what is important about them is that they all focus on proper names, not just nouns. Each of these theories has arguments against it, but then that is acceptable given the fact that all these are theories that come from scholars that come from different persuasions. Additional theories that are equally in the realm of linguistics that informed this researcher are the speech act theory as well as pragmatics.

According to a simple descriptivist theory of anthroponyms, names can be thought of on the following terms or conditions: for every proper name p, there is some assemblage of descriptions D associated with p that establish the meaning of p. For example, the descriptivist may hold that the proper name *Charles Mungoshi* is synonymous with the collection of descriptions such as:

1. the man who wrote the Shona novel *Ndiko Kupindana Kwemazuva*
2. a person who was born in 1940, in Manyene near Chivhu (formerly Enkledoorn)
3. he was educated at St. Augustine's Mission (also known as *kwaTsambe*), at Penhalonga near the eastern border City of Mutare etc. ...

From the above, it is clear that the descriptivist naming theory takes the meaning of the name *Charles Mungoshi* to be that collection of descriptions and it does take the referent of the name to be the thing or object that satisfies all or most of those descriptions.[1]

The other theory is the syntactic one. According to this theory proper names are not the same with proper nouns, but are two entities that are discernible. As propounded by this theory, a proper noun is a word-level unit of the category *noun*, while proper names are noun phrases (syntagms) (Payne and Huddleston 2002: 516). A good illustration of the syntagm is the proper name 'Michael Jackson' or 'Jacob Zuma'. Each of these two examples is made up of two proper nouns: 'Michael' and 'Jackson' as well as 'Jacob' and 'Zuma' respectively. Proper names that are also known as anthroponyms as has already been stated above may also consist of other parts of speech, too. According to the Stanford University website[2] 'Brooklyn Bridge' contains the

---

[1] http://en.wikipedia.org/wiki/Descriptivist_theory_of_names.
[2] http://plato.stanford.edu/entries/names/

common noun 'Bridge' as well as the proper noun 'Brooklyn'. 'The Raritan River' also includes the determiner 'the'. 'The Bronx' combines a determiner and a proper noun. Finally, this theory points out that 'the Golden Gate Bridge' is a proper name with no proper nouns in it at all.

Despite the fact that any string of words (or non-words) can be a proper name, it is possible to (tentatively) locate that openness in the form of proper nouns. It is important to comment on the fact that proper names, by dissimilarity, simply have a large number of paradigms corresponding to the sorts of things named (Carroll 1985 cited in the Stanford website). The website goes on to also state that official names of persons in most Western cultures consist of at least first and last names. These names are also proper nouns in themselves. These are also called in the same Western cultures Christian names, even though there may be nothing Christian or religious about them. There are also cases of names of bridges that have an optional definite determiner and these often contain the common noun 'bridge'. For this reason it is possible to have bridge names that have embedded in them other proper names like 'The George Washington Bridge'. According the Stanford university website it is also possible to in addition have structurally ambiguous and hazy names like 'the New New York Public Library' or in Zimbabwe 'the New National Sports Stadium' even if the stadium is no longer new and is in some cases in need of extensive renovations.

Even if according to the rules of the English language names are often (Geurts 1997; Anderson 2007) claimed to be syntactically "definite," because they can occur with markers of definiteness, like the definite article in English, that rule has exceptions when it comes to Shona and other African

11

languages. Even though definite expressions may include pronouns, demonstratives and definite descriptions, this evidence that is used to support views on which names are subsumed to one of these categories (Larson and Segal 1995; Elbourne 2005) in the English language as in I, Jacob does not *always* hold water in Shona. The word *always* is deliberately italicized because there are certain situations when pronouns or demonstratives do appear with names as in *iye Takunda* (Him Takunda). When people speak as in the given example, they will be emphasizing the importance of Takunda in the issue that is being discussed.

Although the description theory has managed to put some light on the nature and function of names, it has shortcomings, some of which that have been raised by scholars like Kripke in his modal argument (1980: 48-9) (cited in the Stanford University website). In his argument, Kripke's is of the opinion that names and definite descriptions differ in their "modal profiles." His main assertion is that names are *rigid designators*. What he means by this is that their intension is constant across metaphysically possible worlds (where defined). Definite descriptions like 'the author of *Ndiko Kupindana Kwemazuva*,' on the other hand, have non-constant intensions. Kripke strongly supports this taxonomy of his with intuitions about 'might have' modal sentences (taken in the "ontic" or "metaphysical" rather than the epistemic sense).

There is also the semantic theory that relates to names and naming patterns. One of the major semantic theorists is J. S. Mill whose theory is also called Millianism. It is J.S. Mill who is credited (and naming rights) for the common sense view that the semantic contribution of a name is its referent (and only its referent). It is argued that for instance, that the semantic worth of the name 'Aristotle' is Aristotle himself (note that this assumes that, by 'Aristotle', a particular, as opposed to a generic, name is intended). It is highly improbable that Mill was the first person to hold this view. The reason for this assertion is that Mill's argument that a town could still with propriety be called 'Dartmouth' even though it did not lie at the mouth of the Dart River engages with a dialectic that is as old as Plato's *Cratylus*, which underwent a revival in the second half of the twentieth century, beginning with Ruth Barcan Marcus in 1961.[3]

J.S. Mills' theory has itself not without criticism. There is the puzzle of 'the Morning Star' and 'the Evening Star' that Frege's presents as he challenges the Millian conception of names. It is in this case essential to explain that while Frege used 'proper name' [*Eigenname*] to cover singular terms generally, both expressions seem to be proper names of a sort – "star" names. It can also be observed that while both expressions have the same referent (the planet Venus), they do not seem to contribute in the same way to the content of sentences in which they occur. In particular, they cannot be substituted as preserving truth in the scope of propositional attitude verbs. The example that helps clarify Frege's theory is:

1. Homer believed that the Morning Star was the Morning Star. (True)
2. Homer believed that the Morning Star was the Evening Star. (False)

A proposition as the one made by Frege has its own prerequisite conditions and according to Russell (1911) it is a requirement that a propositional attitude holder be acquainted

---

[3] http://plato.stanford.edu/entries/names/

with each of the components of the proposition in question. This Fregian suggestion presents a further problem for the Millian view, for it seems that one can believe the proposition expressed by means of the sentence 'Aristotle was wise' without personally being acquainted with Aristotle, suggesting that Aristotle is not himself contributed to that proposition.[4]

Even if one is to find Russell's epistemological views not persuasive, names without a referent (e.g. Masvingo', Zimbabwe's oldest western urban settlement) create a problem for Millianism. For it is plausible when the Zimbabwean scenario is analysed to note that the sentence 'Masvingo lies due south of Harare' expresses a proposition. This one is distinct from that expressed by 'Chiadzwa lies due east of Masvingo', for someone might believe the former without believing the latter) and yet on the Millian view 'Masvingo' does not contribute anything to the semantic content of the sentence (and certainly nothing over and above what 'Chiadzwa' might contribute). Frege's (1952) sense theories help to provide an answer to his own puzzle because he adds an additional tier, of *Sinn* or "sense," to the referential semantic value of a name. While 'the Morning Star' and 'the Evening Star' have the same reference, or ground-floor semantic value, the expressions differ at the level of sense. The problem that is with Frege's theory is that he left his notion of sense somewhat obscure. Succeeding theorists and scholars have identified a theoretical role that unifies several diverse functions (cf. Kripke 1980: 59; Burge 1977: 356 cited on the Stanford University website). The first observable issue is that an expression has a sense (along with a *Bedeutung* or reference) as part of its semantic value. Its sense is its contribution to the thought (proposition) that is

---

[4] http://plato.stanford.edu/entries/names/

expressed by a sentence in which it occurs. Names, which in this case are considered as generic syntactic types, most likely do not have senses as their linguistic meanings. It is however, important to note that any successful use of a generic name (or perhaps any "particular" name) will express a complete sense. It has to carry a meaning or significance. The second is that the sense of an expression determines its reference. The third aspect is that sense encapsulates the cognitive significance of an expression. In the last capacity, the sense of a sentence – a thought (proposition) – must obey Frege's intuitive criterion of difference (Evans 1982). What this means is that generally, any two sentences that may simultaneously be held to have opposite truth-values by the same rational agent must express different thoughts.

The proposition that Frege makes can be taken further, for example the cited cases of 'the Morning Star' and 'the Evening Star'. In addition to referring to the planet Venus, each of these names has a sense. The sense in each case determines (perhaps with respect to some parameter) the referent Venus. In addition, the senses that comes out put in a nutshell the cognitive significance of each expression. The implication of this realization is that the senses of the two names are different, since the thought expressed by (3) is distinct from the thought expressed by (4) (from the intuitive criterion of difference, and the fact that someone might think (3) is true but (4) is false).

3. The Morning Star is the Morning Star
4. The Morning Star is the Evening Star

There is also another hypothesis that relates to naming which is called the causal-historical theory of reference. Its major proponents are Kripke and Donnellan. These two offer an externalist alternative to the theory that cognitive significance determines reference. Donnellan's main argument is that an "omniscient being that sees the whole history of the affair" is better placed to determine the referent of a particular name than one who limits themselves to the descriptive content associated with the name by a group of agents. The greatest risk as he sees is that the content could be possibly distorted or attenuated. Kripke also suggests that the reference of a name is established by a designation ceremony (or "baptism") at which the object is indicated by a demonstration or uniquely referring description. All uses of the name that derive from this source refer to the original object, even if the speaker associates the name with a description that is untrue of the said object.

Extraordinarily, Kripke himself admits that his irregular description does provide something less than an unquestionable theory. In one very good example, Evans (1973 http://plato.stanford.edu/entries/names/) brings up the noticeable case of 'Madagascar'. He notes that originally the term was used to refer to a portion of mainland Africa, but this important reference shifted to the island that was later colonized by the French off the south eastern coast of Africa. This came about as a result of a miscommunication disseminated and spread by Marco Polo. Notwithstanding the fact that there is a continuous "chain" of derived uses of the name 'Madagascar' going back to the beginning of the mainland, the name as used to date refers to an island. It is clear therefore that the determinants of a name are more complex than Kripke's simplified account would allow.

The above theories clearly point out the fact that it is difficult to come up with a theory of how names are given and the function of names in people's lives. May be the best explanation of the function and importance of names among blacks on the African continent is that given by Asante who states:

What must be done to make it clear that a particular child is being called or asked for when the parent has more than one child? There has to be a way to make this distinction. Humans conceived of the naming process as a way to deal with distinctions (2007: 18).

From Asante's point of view, names are important because they help to establish distinctions between individuals. While they readily do that it is also important to note that another distinction that a name may carry may not be about separating two different individuals. Names can also reflect the perceptions or persuasions of those who name or those who are named. For example, some names may assist one to know whether one is a Christian or not although this has become difficult in some parts of today's world where some people are of different heritages as reflected in their parentage.

While the above theories relate to names and naming, another linguistics theory that is significant to this study is the Speech Act Theory (SAT). The Speech Act Theory was first propounded by Austin. It was later revisited by Grice and Searle. According to SAT all utterances have both a propositional meaning (they say things) and a force (they do things). In this theory Austin distinguishes three kinds of acts an utterance simultaneously performs:

• Locutionary act: The utterance of a sentence with determinate sense and reference. (E.g. I will come back.)

- Illocutionary act: the making of a statement, offer, promise etc. in uttering a sentence, by virtue of the conventional force associated with it. (E.g. a promise or a threat etc.)
- Perlocutionary act: bringing about effects on the audience by means of uttering the sentence, such effects being special to the circumstances of utterances. (E.g. making hearer happy, angry, or scared etc.)

It is important to note that in the most practical sense, the term speech act has largely come to refer exclusively to the illocutionary act.[5] The theory of Austin attracted some response. Some of the scholars who made contributions to it are Searle and Grice. Searle's focus was mainly on the classification of Austin's Speech Acts. He presented them thus:

- Representatives: commit the speaker to the truth of the expressed propositions (e.g. asserting, concluding).
- Directives: attempt by the speaker to get the hearer to do something (e.g. request, question).
- Commissives: commit the speaker to some future course of action (e.g. promise, offer, threat).
- Expressives: express a psychological state (e.g. thanks, apologies, welcome, and congratulation).
- Declarations/Declaratives: effect changes in the institutional state of affairs (e.g., declaring war, christening).

Although Grice's study is on pragmatics, it also shades some light on Austin's SAT. His main aim was to understand

---

[5]

www.coli.unisaarland.de/courses/pragmatics07/Slides/PD.07.3.SpeechActs.pdf

how a "speaker's meaning" i.e. what someone uses an utterance to mean, arises from a sentence's meaning, i.e. the literal form and meaning of an utterance. According to Grice many aspects of a "speaker's meaning" are a consequence of the assumption that the participants in a conversation expect each other to be cooperating. It is this idea of cooperation that Grice in his study of speech acts has called the Cooperative Principle.[6] This cooperative principle that he identified is made up of four sub-parts or maxims that cooperative conversationalists assume each other to be respecting. These are:

- *The maxim of quality.* Speakers' contributions ought to be true.
- *The maxim of quantity.* Speakers' contributions should be as informative as required; not saying either too little or too much.
- *The maxim of relevance.* Contributions should relate to the purposes of the exchange.
- *The maxim of manner.* Contributions should be perspicuous – in particular, they should be tidy, methodical and brief, avoiding obscurity in addition to ambiguity.[7]

It is important to note that Grice was not acting as a prescriptivist when he enunciated these maxims, even though they may sound prescriptive. Rather, he was using observations of the difference between "what is said" and "what is meant" to show that people actually do follow these maxims in conversation.

---

[6] http://people.brandeis.edu/~smalamud/ling100/outline12.pdf
[7] http://people.brandeis.edu/~smalamud/ling100/outline12.pdf

From what is given above that relates to SAT, it is clear according to its assumption that:

- All utterances serve to express propositions and to perform actions
- The (illocutionary) speech act is associated by convention with the form of the utterance
- Illocutionary force is specified by a set of felicity conditions which may be classified according to Searle as:
  - preparatory conditions: real-world prerequisites
  - propositional content conditions
  - sincerity conditions: restriction on beliefs, feelings and intentions of Speaker
- Felicity conditions specify how the context has to be in order for an utterance to perform the type of act it is conventionally associated with.

The illocutionary force is an aspect of meaning that cannot be explained in terms of T or F. It indicates what the addressee is to do with the proposition expressed by the sentence (e.g. believe it, make it true) and must therefore be explained by a theory of action (not a theory of truth-conditional meaning). A study of Shona names as will be found in the discussion that follows below highlights the fact that Shona sentential anthroponyms are Speech Acts in that they are representatives, directives, declaratives, commissives and expressives. They also fulfil Grice's notion of the cooperative principle given the fact that they meet the criteria that is given in the four maxims, that is of quality, quantity, relevance and manner.

Review of Related Literature

This study is not the first one that focuses on Shona names, be they of human beings or flora and fauna. Several researches have been carried out on the Shona name. Only a few of these publications will be discussed in this section. These publications are not necessarily discussed in a chronological order. In 2009, Nyota, Mutasa and Mapara published an article whose main focus was beer hall names that the Shona give either as patrons or as people who look down upon the activities that take place in such places. Among the earliest publications that deal with Shona names is an article by one former Native Commissioner, called Jackson who published in the *Native Affairs Department Annual (NADA)* the article 'The Names of the vaShona' (1957: 116-22). There have been other several publications on Shona names prominent among them being Pongweni's *What's in a Name?: A Study of Shona Nomenclature* (1983). The main thrust of Pongweni's study is names found in Zvarevashe's novels, especially *Kurauone* (1976) and *Gonawapotera* (1978). He also delves into the names of some of the guerrillas who had just come back from Zimbabwe's war of liberation. But like Jackson (1957), Nyota, Mutasa and Mapara (2009) Pongweni mixes the different types of names that he discusses. He has as well largely focused on Karanga names.

Pfukwa (2012) has focused on *Chimurenga* (Zimbabwean War of Liberation) names in his *A Dictionary of Chimurenga War Names*. His research which is anchored in his doctoral thesis complements what Pongweni wrote on in *What's in a Name?: A Study of Shona Nomenclature* (1983). In this dictionary, Pfukwa handles issues such as the essence of Chimurenga names, heroism and the potential beneficiaries of his dictionary. Earlier on in 2007, Pfukwa also researched on *Chimurenga* names. But like all the writers on names, he as well did not focus on sentential names. While he dwelt on these, they are covered under the umbrella of guerrilla names. They have no section or chapter of their own that they belong to. In fact, Pfukwa's writings on names discuss different types of names, some which are Shona, some English and others that are a combination of both Shona and English. Another recent work that focuses on names is that by Makondo. In 2009, Makondo submitted his doctoral thesis on Shona anthroponyms to the University of South Africa. What sets apart the two works (Makondo and Pongweni) is that Pongweni's book does not only focus on human names but also on dog names that Mapara and Nyota (2011) as well as Mapara and Thebe in a forthcoming publication that was initially presented at the LASU conference call canonyms.

George Kahari has also published on Shona names. Earlier on in 1986, and 1990 he had published on the categories into which Shona names can be classified. The categories that Kahari comes up with are all circumstantial. According to Kahari, the Shona are named following these identified typologies: *zita remudumba* (maternity home name), *zita regombwa* (name associated with one's ancestral spirits), *zita rejemedzwa* (the diviner's suggested name) and *zita redzinza* (lineage name). These he puts in category A. In category B there are: *zita remadunhurirwa* (nickname), *zita rechihani* (associative name that marks a family's social or historical event) and *zita rechenza* (a name that means to act or follow the example of someone) (Kahari 1990: 282-3). Kahari like Makondo is focusing on human names only, but specifically on how one's immediate environment informs how one names as well as what name or names to give to a child or even him or herself as the war of liberation names that some guerrillas bore in this war that was fought between 1966 and 1979 when a ceasefire came into effect after the Lancaster House Conference. Kahari is also interested in identifying typologies of Shona names. In their 2011 publication, *Shona Names as Communication and Description: A Case of the Manyika*, Mapara, Nyota and Mutasa also discuss names that they see as being summaries of the people who bear them or of the circumstances that surround them, be they positive or negative. The gap that this study sought to fill was the one that is more on the linguistic front than one that relates to human beings or animals only. Mapara, Nyota and Mutasa's publication is a combination of anthroponyms and toponyms, while this study is entirely on people's names. This study does also not focus on the typologies similar to the ones that Kahari (1990) has given. It again does not fill the categories that Kahari has identified. What the study has done is to compress all of Kahari's categories into one linguistic one and its focus is on names that are sentences, which this writer and researcher calls sentential names. By sentential names the researcher means names that are complete sentences in the form of questions or statements but are complete in them appearing with or without a subject but being a clause on their own.

Research Design and Methods

This research used the qualitative approach. Key (1997: 1) posits that the term qualitative research is a generic term that is used to refer to investigative inquiry procedures that can best be described as ethnographic, naturalistic, anthropological, field, or participant observer investigation.

Kirk and Miller (in Gall, Borg and Gall 1996: 547) add on to this observation and define qualitative research as an approach to social sciences that involves watching people in their own territory and interacting with them in their own language and on their own terms. Gall, Borg and Gall (1996: 547) also note that the qualitative approach involves fieldwork in which the researcher interacts with the study participants in their own environment. This act of observation is significant because it gives the researcher room to gather primary data since s/he will be interacting with the subjects of study on a one-to-one basis. Dees (1993: 92-3) buttresses the importance of this approach when he states that it among other things enables the researcher to record behaviour, describe conditions and examine primary material.

This was the approach that was therefore considered to be important because as Denzin (1989: 83) perceives, qualitative research goes beyond mere fact and external appearances. He notes that it presents detail, context, emotion and the webs of social relationships that join people to each other. The qualitative method establishes the importance of an experience, or the sequence of events, for the person or persons in question. As a method it accentuates the significance of looking at variables in their natural setting in which they are found. Comprehensive data is collected through open ended questions that help provide direct quotations.

The qualitative research approach is also essential because it searches for answers to questions and systematically uses a predefined set of procedures to answer the questions, collects evidence as well as in addition producing findings that are applicable beyond the immediate boundaries of the study. Additionally, it seeks to understand a given research problem or topic from the perspectives of the local population it involves. Qualitative research is especially effective in obtaining culturally specific information about the values, opinions, behaviours, and social contents of particular populations. It was therefore found to be relevant for this study because names are cultural.

The strength of qualitative research lies in its capability to provide complex textual descriptions of how people experience a given research issue. Qualitative methods are also effective in identifying intangible factors, such as social norms, socio-economic and political status, gender roles, ethnicity, and religion, whose role in the research issue may not be readily apparent. The advantages of the qualitative research approach are also that it produces more in-depth and comprehensive information as well as use subjective information and participant observation to describe the context, or natural setting, of the variables under consideration, as well as the interactions of the different variables in the context when compared to the quantitative one. It seeks a wide understanding of the entire situation.

Cohen, Manion and Morrison (2011: 537) also remark that qualitative data derives from many sources that include but are not limited to the following: interviews, observation, field notes, documents and reports, memos, emails and online conversations, diaries, audio and video as well film materials, website data, advertisements and print material, pictures and photographs and artefacts. Best and Khan agree with these scholars and dwell at length on the qualitative research approach and its methods (1993: 183-204).

Wolcott (1990) goes on to state that methods of maintaining the validity of qualitative research for the researcher are that she or he be a good listener, record accurately, initiate writing early, include the primary data in the final report, include all data in the primary report, be candid, seek feedback, attempt to achieve balance, in addition to writing accurately.

Despite its advantages, the qualitative approach also has its disadvantages. These are that the very subjectivity of the inquiry leads to difficulties in establishing the reliability and validity of the approaches and information. It is also very difficult to prevent or detect researcher induced bias.

The study was carried out in Nyanga and Mutasa districts in Manicaland Province in eastern Zimbabwe in December 2010, April 2011 and April 2012. The reason for identifying the research areas was because the two districts were very much influenced by the high levels of guerrilla penetration during Zimbabwe's war of liberation. The two districts are also home to several Christian denominations such as the Anglicans, Roman Catholics, United Methodists and Pentecostals as well as followers of African Initiated Churches such as the Johane Marange apostolic sect that has its origins in the Mafararikwa area of Bocha and Guta RaJehova (GRJ) of Mai Chaza that has its base outside the City of Mutare in Zimunya. Besides these factors, the same districts also have many practitioners of African Traditional Religions (ATRs). All these events and practices have a lot of influences that they have brought to bear on the naming practices as well as the names that some people came across during the war of liberation.

This is a cultural research and it is qualitative. The advantage of using the qualitative research model is that it is flexible since it allows the researcher to use the natural setting, and not a laboratory. It is an interactive type of research. In this study the researcher relied on observing some naming practices within certain situations, informal interviews and discussions. He opted for this approach because it is interactive and it is done in a relaxed manner (Kombo and Tromp 2006: 9). The study falls within the realm of ethnographic study in that its main focus is on a particular group or groups who in this case are the Manyika found in Mutasa and Nyanga districts of Manicaland Province. The research sought to analyse the naming behaviour of a particular group of people in different circumstances and also how they responded to names that came from outside as the guerrillas descended onto their homes in search of logistical support as well as for purposes of educating the masses on the importance of the war of liberation and why it was necessary that the war be fought. This they did as they crossed into Zimbabwe from neighbouring Mozambique between 1974 and 1979, when the war itself came to an end when the warring parties came to an agreement to end the war and resolve their political differences through the ballot box.

Conceptual Hypothesis

The environment within which people live influences the way they name their children, relatives or themselves. That environment gives them room to define or redefine themselves. They do this by giving names that are hanging words or are sentences. Sentential names therefore come about as a result of people wishing to make statements that relate to social, political or religious matters. But then what is a sentence?

27

Definition of a sentence

A sentence is difficult to define but it can be briefly described as a grammatical component that is composed of one or more clauses that conglomerate to make sense grammatically.[8] Chalker and Weiner (1994: 358) also go on to define a sentence as the largest element of language structure that is in traditional grammar treated as having a subject and a predicate. It is also defined as a set of words that express a complete thought. Chalker and Weiner (1994: 358) further remark that it is not always the case that all sentences have a subject and a predicate. This insight is very important as the two writers go on to give the example of imperatives that usually have no expressed subject. A good example in Shona can be the imperative clause, *Buda muno*! (Get out!) Some sentences are also elliptical and this means the definition of a sentence taking into consideration the issue of ellipsis is something that can be expanded to consist of elliptical material and non-productive items.[9] It is important to note that the word *elliptical* refers to the concept of *ellipsis* which means leaving something out of a sentence. The following examples clearly highlight what elliptical sentences are:

- *Unonzi ani?* (What is your name?)
- *Takunda*
- *Unobva kupi?* (Where do you come from?)
- *Nyanga*

---

[8] www.sil.org/linguistics/GlossaryOfLinguisticTerms/WhatIsASentence.htm
[9] www.sil.org/linguistics/GlossaryOfLinguisticTerms/WhatIsASentence.htm

A look at the above examples makes it clear that the words *Takunda* and *Nyanga* are elliptical sentences which are given as responses to the questions asked. Instead of saying *Ndinonzi Takunda* (My name is Takunda) the respondent only gives out his name. In the dialogue that the two sides are having it is assumed that the other part knows that the other part of the statement that is not spoken because of the context, but it is there. The term sentential therefore means being or pertaining to a sentence or sentences (Chalker and Weiner 1994: 360).

Aim of the study

The aim of this study was to investigate the factors that influence the Shona, specifically the Manyika to give the names that they decide to give to their children as first names or to neighbours, relatives and friends as nicknames. The main focus of the aim was not just on names that carry meanings but anthroponyms that also assume the status of sentences because they come out as complete statements in themselves. Some of these names also raise eyebrows when they are called out because in some instances some hearers wonder at what messages the namers would have wanted to bring out. One other aim of the study was to bring to the attention of scholars as well as other readers the fact that names are not innocent labels, but that to understand some names also means to have some insight into some cultural practices. The most important issue relating to this study is that the researcher sought to bring to the attention of readers the fact that some name bearers become living symbols and statements of the names that they carry. This is very much true of those who bear sentential names.

29

Objectives of the study

When the study was carried out, the following are some of the objectives that the researcher sought to establish and these objectives were to:

- Determine the social factors that inform the Shona in their naming practices.
- Establish whether the so-called Christian names that the Shona give their children are really Christian or they fall within the realm of African Traditional Religions (ATRs).
- To find out the main reasons why those who gave themselves or were given *noms de guerre* believe(d) in the significance of the names that they carried or they were being used as a cover against the Rhodesian forces in the case of Zimbabwe's war of liberation.

Limitations and scope of the study

The study only focused on the Shona and specifically the Manyika of Nyanga and Mutasa districts. It is only limited to the study of human names and not those given to dogs, cattle or other animals although it is generally known among the Shona that some names like *Muchaneta* (You shall tire) do cross the line because they can be found as both human and dog names. The study was also limited to names that are complete statements in themselves or show signs of being elliptical sentences as some of the examples discussed in this study will reveal.

This research is made up of six chapters. The first chapter is the introduction. It gives a brief background on how the study came about. Among other issues that it discusses are aspects such as methods of research, theoretical framework, aims, objectives and the review of related literature. The second chapter is titled 'Names as Heritage and Cultural Expressions'. In this chapter the researcher sought to give a grounding of Shona names in a cultural context where they are looked at as part of the heritage that the long departed generations bequeathed to today's progeny. The heritage aspect is also significant because it acts as a wakeup call to the Shona and other Zimbabweans at large as well as other formerly colonised people to really redefine themselves as a people who own their own destiny and not be a people who are owned and thus controlled by others. In short, the chapter says that renaming oneself is a way of reclaiming one's identity which is part and parcel of the decolonising process.

In chapters three to five the writer discusses the names that were sampled. Chapter three of this research focuses on the socio-cultural environment and how this influences the naming patterns of a particular group. It is aptly titled 'The Socio-cultural names of the Manyika.' In the fifth chapter the study discusses religious names that the Manyika under the influence of the Christian faith, both Pentecostal and Traditional (that is Catholic and Protestant) are giving to their children, or names that they assume after converting to this faith. It is titled 'Some Shona Theophoric Sentential Anthroponyms'.

The fifth chapter discusses a special category of names – *Chimurenga* names. These are special because they usually come once in a historical period. It is not normal for nations to again wage another war of liberation after another one has been fought and they have attained independence. Any war after that of liberation is called civil war or by any other name. Names that the guerrillas involved in this fight give to themselves no longer qualify to be called liberation war names, at least in the case of Zimbabwe because the term *Chimurenga/Imfazo* (Uprising) is associated with the fight against colonialism and counter to the continued rule of the whites as a minority.

The conclusion of the research comes in chapter six. In this chapter the researcher does not only close the research but also discusses his major findings in as far as the naming practice of sentential names is concerned.

Conclusion

This chapter has discussed among other issues the area of research, the methods of research as well as the research design. It has discussed the importance of these to the study. One other area that the chapter has highlighted is the one that relates to the naming patterns of the Shona. Besides giving a brief overview of the literature that is there that relates to names and naming practices among the Shona, the study has as well delved into an exposition of why this study was necessary. It has noted that most people have opinions that perceive some Shona names, especially sentential ones in the negative. It has argued that this should not be the case. The next chapter discusses the sentential names in the context of heritage given the fact that they are part and parcel of a practice that this era's progeny has inherited from the generations of yesteryear.

Chapter II

Shona Names as Heritage and Cultural Expressions

Introduction

Names fall under several categories. Linguistically they are parts of speech. As labels that help to identify objects or human beings they belong to the realm of language study. But besides that names also have another interesting dimension to them. It is important to realise that the practice of naming whether they be objects or human beings is something that has been with human generations since time immemorial. That means that the practice of naming is one that has been bequeathed to today's people by past generations. It is not something that is peculiar to a particular ethnic group or race. It is universal. The fact that today's generation have retained it means that it is part of the heritage they want to be perpetuated and sustained because of its value to humanity. While it is acknowledged that the practice of naming has been handed down to all humanity by past generations, some naming practices are dying due to external influences such as western cultural goods that come in the form of fiction works as well as films. They have also been affected by the Christian faith, especially main stream Christian denominations such as the Roman Catholic and Anglican Churches that have tended to advise their converts and followers to assume new names, especially those of saints at baptism and confirmation. The effect of this has been the erosion of the Shona heritage of giving to children names that relate to the family and parents' immediate environment. It is important to note that Shona names just like any other, as well as the environment that informs their coming into being are part of the general heritage of the African people in as a broad-spectrum and the Shona, specifically the Manyika in particular. It is in the light of this that the word heritage as it relates to names needs to be unpacked because to some people, the term heritage means other things that are not names such as monuments that are part of the tangible cultural heritage and songs as well as some other practices that they accept and acknowledge to be intangible cultural heritage.

Heritage

Heritage is something that is passed down from one generation to another; a tradition, custom or customs that those who have received them consider to be important. It is a way of doing things. Heritage refers to practices such as naming that the present generations have inherited from the past. The United Nations Scientific and Cultural Organisation (UNESCO) is also very illuminating in this area and it thus defines heritage as:

> ... our legacy from the past, what we live with today and what we pass on to future generations. Our cultural and natural heritage are both irreplaceable sources of life and inspiration.[10]

This definition is very broad. It encompasses a lot of things that include the tangible and the intangible. Although this definition does not make any reference to names or

---

[10] http://www.whc.unesco.org/en/about

34

naming practices, the researcher would like to highlight its significance which is embraced in the words "our legacy from the past". Each group of people or clan has practices either living or dead that that have been handed down through the generations that have been useful in informing parents in naming their children. These practices are therefore part of each people's cultural heritage. They are also important because they give some insights into family and clan history. So to choose to name in a manner that is foreign is to throw away one's history. It is equivalent to rejecting oneself and thus a failure on one's part to acknowledge his or her existence as a human being.

The University of Massachusetts website also gives more insights into what heritage is. According to this website, heritage is a full range of a people's inherited traditions, monuments, objects and culture, with the most important part of the heritage being meanings and behaviours that contemporary society derives from them. This same website adds on that heritage includes among other things, the following: preserving, excavating, displaying or restoring a collection of old things or artefacts. It is important to note that heritage is however, not limited to these things. It is in two categories, and these are tangible and intangible heritage. Intangible heritage is fully manifested in the tangible. This means that it is pointless to talk of one type of heritage without talking about the other. Intangible heritage includes ideas as well as memories of various things that include songs, dances, games, recipes, language and many other elements that help in reflecting on the identity of a particular group of people.[11]

---

[11] http://www.umass.edu/chs/about/whatisheritage.html

It is important to realize that prior to the categorization of heritage into either tangible or intangible, the earlier definitions have always focused on the tangible especially sites and monuments. This comes out clearly in the 1972 UNESCO Convention on World Heritage. According to this Convention:

For the purposes of this Convention, the following shall be considered as 'cultural heritage':

Monuments: architectural works, works of monumental sculpture and painting, elements or structures of an archaeological nature,, inscriptions, cave dwellings and combinations of features, which are of outstanding universal value from the point of view of history, art or science;

groups of buildings; groups of separate or connected buildings which, because of their architecture, their homogeneity or their place in the landscape, are of outstanding universal value from the point of view of history, art or science;

sites: works of man or the combined works of nature and of man, and areas including archaeological sites which are of outstanding universal value from the historical, aesthetic, ethnological or anthropological points of view.

A look at the above definition shows that this definition was informed more by a Eurocentric view than one that is inclusive. This definition falls short in the area of practices that even when applied to western situations, could have led to the erection of such buildings and monuments as well as the use of certain sites for definite functions. It is therefore plausible that the 2003 Convention on Intangible Cultural

Heritage came into being. This one recognizes practices among other things and it defines cultural heritage thus:

For the purposes of this Convention,

1. The "intangible cultural heritage" means the practices, representations, expressions, knowledge, skills – as well as the instruments, objects, artefacts and cultural spaces associated therewith – that communities, groups and, in some cases, individuals recognize as part of their cultural heritage. This intangible cultural heritage, transmitted from generation to generation, is constantly recreated by communities and groups in response to their environment, their interaction with nature and their history, and provides them with a sense of identity and continuity, thus promoting respect for cultural diversity and human creativity. For the purposes of this Convention, consideration will be given solely to such intangible cultural heritage as is compatible with existing international human rights instruments, as well as with the requirements of mutual respect among communities, groups and individuals, and of sustainable development.

2. The "intangible cultural heritage", as defined in paragraph 1 above, is manifested inter alia in the following domains: (a) oral traditions and expressions, including language as a vehicle of the intangible cultural heritage; (b) performing arts; (c) social practices, rituals and festive events; (d) knowledge and practices concerning nature and the universe; (e) traditional craftsmanship.

This definition is more inclusive. A detailed study of it will reveal that the art of naming among the Manyika falls under practices and expressions and as the second part of the definition highlights, naming practices fall under both (a) and (c). Names belong to the category of oral traditions and expressions and included in these is language that is seen as a vehicle of the intangible cultural heritage. They also fall under social practices in that any naming act is performed in a social environment, whether that is political or religious. It is therefore acceptable that names fall under heritage, and qualify to be defined so because as already observed in the discussion above one other aspect of the intangible cultural heritage is the naming practices of a given people. One essential and significant aspect of each people's heritage and that relates to the preserving of heritage is therefore the names that people give to themselves, their children or peers but that are peculiar to that group. It is important to note that when people name in their own language and from their own culture and traditions, they are not only celebrating their being. They are also preserving and promoting their heritage, a thing that is promoted by UNESCO as stated in the 2003 Convention on Intangible Cultural Heritage. As has already been highlighted above, to name in a language that is not one's own is the greatest form of self-betrayal and self-hate. This was possible in the era of colonialism but to continue to do that today is very unforgivable. People have to learn to redefine and reassert themselves in this global village, and one way of doing that is through giving culturally significant names.

Names as Heritage and Memory

While the above section has handled the issue of heritage it has to be observed that names themselves are heritage items. As heritage forms names are a means of communication. This is important because not all people use similar communication channels. Despite advances in the use of technology that has seen even the use of cell phones, and of late i-pads, it is equally significant to make note on the realisation that some people still use names to communicate and express their joys, sorrows or tribulations.

Names are also important as heritage because those that do have meanings and are given in the indigenous language of those who name and they also carry their history or portions of their history. In addition to that, names are also significant as memory centres. It is essential to note that besides carrying the histories of families and clans, their contribution to heritage is realized when it is noted that some sentential names do carry with them memories of the pains that some people or families would have gone through in their journey of life. An example of a name that has a mnemonic function is *Ndaizivei* (What did I know?/ I knew nothing) where the namer is stating that s/he fell into problems because of lack of knowledge or in some instances lack of adequate knowledge. The knowledge may have been that to do with information that would have led him/her to make informed decisions before getting involved in whatever activities that finally led him/her into the predicament that led to the giving of that name to a child born after the event.

As heritage, names also tell the history and practices of particular peoples. Examples of such names are *Mhandamabwe* and *Mahwemasimike*. These two are names of places that in linguistics and cultural geography are called toponyms. The first name refers to a place in Chivi district in Masvingo Province in Zimbabwe. The second one is the name of two twin peaks that are found in Honde Valley in Mutasa district, Manicaland Province in eastern Zimbabwe. *Mhandamabwe* is a descriptive name. It describes a place that is so rocky that according to the legend in Masvingo Province, one has to crack stones so as to be able to plant crops. The same legend states that that is why there is the Shona proverb that says, *Zvinhu zviedzwa, chembere yekwaChivi yakabika mabwe ikaseva muto* (Some things are worth trying, an old woman from Chivi cooked some stones and she got some broth from them). This name is significant in that it highlights the plight of some of the people who stay in Chivi district. They have very little and also no arable land in some instances. In fact, if one was to visit the place, the evidence of a rock area that is largely covered in stones is there. The other name, *Mahwemasimike* is equally descriptive. While *Mhandamabwe* describes the terrain, the latter describes the twin peaks that to the ordinary eye appear to have been planted. It is because of their appearance that they are given this name. These two names are a clear indication that names are part of a people's heritage. It is a tradition or custom that has been bequeathed to the Shona of today that toponyms (place names) can at times be given as a result of the communities being informed by their immediate environment, in this case it being their bio-physical environment.

The above paragraph has already pointed out that the naming of places in a descriptive manner is a practice that relates to geography as well and this is known as cultural geography. The cultural geography of place names is part of heritage. The United Nations' Group of Experts on Geographical Names meeting in Vienna in May 2011 acknowledged the value of some place names as heritage. The experts noted that there is a relationship that exists between cultural heritage and geographic names and they state that this is a significant representation of the identity of ethnic groups with a spatial object in the context of: monuments, squares, artefacts, geographic names of places, landscapes, rivers, waterfalls, mountains, old plantations, infrastructure, industrial heritage, architecture and archaeological sites with petroglyphs. This cultural heritage, they note, is important for the identity of society. It reinforces the culture and self-consciousness of all ethnic groups. The geographical names are therefore a source of inspiration for local, regional and national identity of ethnic groups (United Nations Group of Experts on Geographical Names 2011: 5). One thing that comes out clearly in this group's observation is that geographic names are sources of inspiration to their people. What the group is saying in other words is that geographical names are memory beacons. They are part and parcel of a people's memory.

Memories are part of the identity and history of a people. It is a common practice among the Shona to reflect on the progress or non-progress of the *mhuri* or *dzinza* (family or clan). At times the memories of the good and the bad are captured and memorialized through names. The two examples that follow show names playing this important role:

• *Tadiwanashe* (We have been favoured by the Lord). This name is acknowledging the parents of a child's gratefulness to their Lord may be for the birth of this particular child whom they have been praying for. It is also possible that they may have wanted a baby boy but were always getting girls, now the birth of a boy brings forth happiness and joy hence the declaration that they have been favoured by the Lord.

• *Toitasei* (What shall we do?) This name is in the protesting mode. The parents are protesting maybe against bad neighbours or even family members who could be bothering them. The name can also have political undertones as will be observed later in the chapter that deals with socio-cultural names.

Kahari (1990: 282-3) has equally highlighted the importance of names as memory centres. The types of names that Kahari gives that are linked to memory and heritage are *zita regombwa* (name associated with one's ancestral spirits), *zita rejemedzwa* (a diviner's suggested name), *zita redzinza* (lineage name) and *zita rechihani* (an associative name that is used to mark a family's social or historical event). According to the same scholar, *zita regombwa* is given to a child by a family that wishes to have that child carry on the outstanding exploits of one of its ancestors. This name is given in memory of the departed but also with the intention of inspiring the namesake to be as successful as that one he or she is named after. It does not mean as most Christians would want to believe that the child will become the living host of the long departed ancestor. It is a continued celebration of the exploits of what a family or clan member would have done. This explains why in a given family (read extended family because this concept does not exist among the Shona to whom the Manyika belong) and clan several children can share that same name. This therefore means that the fear of those people who see the namesakes being potential hosts of the long departed are unfounded.

Zita rejemedzwa is linked to the one above, *zita regombwa*. The difference is that this name is given after a child is found to be incessantly crying without any outward signs of illness. When this happens, the parents of the child consult a diviner who may suggest that the child is crying because a departed ancestor would like his/her name to be called on a given

42

child. Even though this name is not the choice of the parents, its significance lies in the fact that it reflects the Shona religious heritage that is looked down upon by western versions of Christianity that require converts to assume what they call 'Christian names'.

Zita redzinza is again in the line of heritage and memory. It is a lineage name that is given to one who takes a new office, in most cases as chief. When he is installed as chief he abandons the use of all other names that he has been hitherto called by. He now assumes a new name and it is this name that becomes his until death. *Zita redzinza* is also a ritual name in that when one is installed into a new office, he is given instructions that have been given to others that have borne that name and have gone before him/her. This practice is similar to that of the English throne where the new queen or king assumes the name of a king or queen who has gone before. The only difference is that a number is appended to the new entrant to the throne, e.g. Elizabeth II. Closer home are the two cases of Lesotho and Swaziland that have Letsie III and Mswati II, son of Sobhuza II.

Zita rechihani is an associative or historical name. It is a name that is given in association with a particular place. It can also be given as a commemoration to a particular event. Kahari sums up this name with reference to the Zimbabwean situation when he states:

> This name is given to a child to recall occurrences or feelings which corresponded to it. Some children born at Independence in Zimbabwe, 1980 are called Independence or Mugabe to mark the occasion.

The example given above shows this type of name being more of historical than associative although there are also children who are given names such as *Muzuva* (In the sun) because their parents always associate their birth with a year of drought, a year when that particular child was born. In all these naming practices that the Shona use, it is evident that they use names to express their thoughts and feelings on certain issues. Names therefore become platforms of cultural expressions.

Kahari's categorization of names is given from a largely Zezuru perspective. In an interview with James Hlongwana on 15 February 2013, the Ndau, a Shona group in South Eastern Zimbabwe have three categories. These are: *zita rekubarwa* (birth name) which is similar to Kahari's *zita remudumba*, *zita reujaha/ undombi* (adolescence name) and *zita reurombo* (name reflecting personal tragedies). *Zita reujaha* or *undombi* is the name that a person in adolescence gives himself largely because s/he would not be comfortable with *zita rekubarwa* which was given by parents. It is an act of onomastic erasure in the sense that the person would be running away from the history and the circumstances that would have led to him or her getting that name. *Zita reurombo* is a name that a person gives him or herself after suffering personal tragedies. For example, a woman who has become a widow, and this widowhood would lead to changes in her lifestyle may give herself a name that would reflect her changed circumstances. She may for example, call herself *Matambudziko* (Sufferings) because she would be living a life that would be characterised by constant suffering that may not only included deprivation but also rejection by her late husband's relatives. They may in addition add to her problems by accusing her of having bewitched their late relative. In short, *zita reurombo* is a statement of the bad experiences one would have gone through. Again like the Manyika, the Ndau also have nicknames, (*zita rekutsvinya*) but what is most significant to them are the types of names that have been discussed earlier. One other type of name that is similar to that given by Kahari is *zita redzinza*. All Shona groups have this name. In fact the surnames that most Shona people carry are lineage names.

It is also interesting to note that while the Manyika do not have *zita reurombo*, they like the Ndau have the other two name types – *rekubarwa* and *reujaha neumhandara*. The only difference is that where the Ndau have *undombi* which is used to refer to a young woman in adolescence, the Manyika have *reumhandara*. At times *zita reujaha/umhandara (undombi)* was given to the bearer by his or her teachers or missionaries and in some instances the local catechists.

Names as Cultural Expressions

It is equally essential to remember that names as intangible cultural heritage are also promoters of cultural diversity as given in the 2005 Convention on the Protection and Promotion of the Diversity of Cultural Expressions. Earlier on in 2001 UNESCO had declared the importance of cultural diversity among humanity. Its Article 1 of the Declaration clearly states that cultural diversity is a common heritage for humanity. The Declaration goes on to confirm and acknowledge that culture manifests itself in diverse forms across time and space. It further recognizes the fact that this diversity of humanity is brought to life in the uniqueness and plurality of the identities of the groups and societies that make up humankind. Cultural diversity is as well accepted in this Declaration as a source of exchange, innovation and creativity, which is as necessary for humankind as biodiversity is for nature. It is in this sense that it has to be accepted and appreciated as the common heritage of humanity that deserves to be recognized and affirmed for the benefit it brings to the present and future generations.

In 2005 UNESCO crafted a convention that highlights the importance of cultural diversity. This convention is very important in this time and age where genocide appears to be the norm. In Africa there has been the recent case of Rwanda. Earlier on between 1939 and 1945 there were Hitler's extermination camps that saw more than six million Jews killed largely through poisoning and after this they were cremated. This Convention in its preamble affirmed that cultural diversity is a defining characteristic of humanity. It also went on to note that it was mindful of the fact that cultural diversity forms a common heritage of humanity and should be cherished and preserved for the benefit of all. The third principle of the same convention goes on to state that the protection and promotion of the diversity of cultural expressions presupposes the recognition of equal dignity of and respect for all cultures, including the cultures of persons belonging to minorities and indigenous peoples. This is very significant. It has always been the cultures of the indigenous whose lands got colonised that have been marginalised. In most cases, the same marginalised people have become minorities. Colonialism in Africa has also minoritised some people because in a given country they are only found as a small group yet in reality they will be more than that since they are cross-border peoples.

A critical study of the three conventions, that of 2003, 2005 and that of 1972 as well as the 2001 Universal Declaration on Cultural Diversity shows that they are complementary. Cultural heritage, whether tangible or intangible cannot thrive and neither can it be appreciated and therefore promoted, safeguarded and preserved in a world that does not cherish diversity and promote it. It is therefore heartening to note that the naming practices of the Manyika reflect and carry this diversity. To deny or speak ill of the manner in which people name their children, relatives and friends is to refuse to acknowledge the diversity that makes up humanity. This unfortunately has been the case in Zimbabwe, especially among the group that is focused in this study. When western Christian denominations came, especially the Roman Catholics, who have their Mission station at Triashill, and the Anglicans who have theirs at St. Augustine's Mission near Penhalonga came, they actively advised their new converts to use 'Christian' names. Pei (1965: 74) re-echoes this imposition by the Church and notes that the Christian Church, especially the Roman Catholic insisted that people use first names which are taken either from the bible or from their calendar of saints. African names were on the other hand labelled as unholy. This reference to African names in such negative terms goes against the spirit of cultural diversity especially when one considers the fact that when the same missionaries first came to Zimbabwe some of them even mooted the idea of destroying Shona traditions that they alleged were having a bad influence on those who wanted to convert to the Christian faith. According to Zvobgo (1986: 50):

The missionaries hoped to destroy African traditions through the ministry of preaching, the translation of the Scriptures into the vernacular, the ministry of healing, the establishment of Christian villages and Western education.

These words point out to the fact that the missionaries opted for the strategy of attrition. The effect of this approach was to slowly but surely destroy the very fabric of the core of what it meant to be African. This approach was a form of genocide. Some argue that the term genocide to be used with reference to the missionaries is too strong a term, but then when the words of Chalk and Jonassohn (quoted in Jones 2011: 4) are analysed, the activities of the missionaries are akin to genocide. The two state:

Historically and anthropologically peoples have always had a name for themselves. In a great many cases, that name meant "the people" to set the owners of that name off against all other people who were considered of lesser quality in some way. If the differences between the people and some other society were particularly large in terms of religion, language manners, customs, and so on, then such others were seen as less than fully human: pagans, savages, or even animals.

Although the missionaries who came to Zimbabwe together with Cecil John Rhodes's British South Africa Company (BSAC) in 1890 were not many, they considered the Shona and the Ndebele whom they came to preach to as less human and a Catholic priest O'Neil stated, "They are hopeless pagans" (quoted in Zvobgo 1986: 50). It is because of them being seen as hopeless that the missionaries saw it fit to have their traditions destroyed (Zvobgo 1986: 50). One of the ways of destroying these traditions was to encourage new converts to assume new names and to also name their children not according to their traditions but according to the new faith that they had been compelled to embrace.

It is important to note that among the Shona, names are not just labels. They carry meanings. As has already been noted above, they also carry the memories of a family or a clan. To therefore ask people to assume new naming patterns as a way of undermining their traditions is also committing a slow type of genocide which is called memoricide. According to Jacques Sémelin, (in Jones 2011: 28) memoricide is the destruction not only of those people who are deemed to be undesirable in a territory to be purified, but also of any traces that might recall their erstwhile presence such as schools, religions and other related sites and monuments. This definition of memoricide tallies with that given in the United Nations Convention on the Prevention and Punishment of the Crime of Genocide of 1948. Article II of the Convention states:

> In the present Convention, genocide means any of the following acts committed with intent to destroy, in whole or in part, a national, ethnical, racial or religious group, as such: a) Killing members of the group; b) Causing serious bodily or mental harm to members of the group; c) Deliberately inflicting on the group conditions of life calculated to bring about its physical destruction in whole or in part; d) Imposing measures intended to prevent births within the group; e) Forcibly transferring children of the group to another group.

Although the bulk of the above definition is on the physical elimination of human beings, item b) says, "Causing serious bodily or mental harm to members of the group". This is very illuminating. The directive that new converts have new names that were western; this in itself is a form of mental harm and therefore constitutes genocide.

Meharg notes that there is another form of the destruction of a people, another form of genocide. This she calls identicide. She argues that the premeditated extermination of a group's identity through the destruction of places, people and practices are the underpinnings of genocide. She further observes that identicide is a strategy of warfare that is deliberately set in motion to target and obliterate cultural symbols and fundamentals through a variety of means in order to contribute to eventual acculturation, removal, and/or total destruction of a particular identity group, including its contested signs, symbols, behaviours, values, places and performances (in Meharg 2006: 9). Even though the church is not in a type of war that can be defined as military, its intention was to destroy among other things the "contested signs, symbols, behaviours, values, places and performances" of the Shona. These include naming practices. It is however interesting to note that despite the onslaught of the church on the Shona and other African traditions, especially the naming ones, these never completely died and the coming of nationalism in the 1950s as well as the war of liberation and independence in 1980 ensured that these naming practices were again revived and have even been accepted by the church.

Conclusion

This chapter has discussed the importance of Shona names and their value as heritage and cultural expressions. It has done this by initially defining what heritage is. The chapter has gone on to discuss and give examples of how names can become part of a people's cultural heritage. It has done this by giving examples of two places, *Mhandamabwe* in Masvingo Province's Chivi district and *Mahwemasimike* in Mutasa district in Manicaland Province. The chapter has also discussed the role of the church in its attempts to impede and destroy the practices of the Shona in its efforts to spread evangelization. It has noted that the church made a deliberate effort to undermine the traditions and practices of the Shona in an effort to ensure that its numbers grew. These attempts as the research has observed were just as bad as genocide because their focus was to destroy the memory of the Shona as well as their identity, since they always stated that any baptized person would come out of baptism a new being. This being new among other things meant the African's loss of his identity and memory. These attempts have been labelled identicide and memoricide. This is so because the activities of the missionaries as the chapter has highlighted were intended to culturally obliterate the Shona. The chapter has as well discussed the factors that led the Shona to give certain names to their children. In addition to that, the chapter has also noted that when a new chief was installed, he assumed a new name, and got a name that reflected his new status as chief of all people and not only of those of his clan. The chapter has also noted that by insisting that blacks get new names and abandon their practices and embrace the Christian faith, the missionaries were going against the spirit of diversity, even though of course at the time of their preaching such Conventions and Declarations as those of 2001 and 2005 were not yet in place. They acted with the arrogance of those who saw themselves as pure and superior. This was the tragedy, not only with the Manyika but with all black Africa. The next chapter discusses the naming practices of the Manyika in a socio-cultural context.

Chapter III

The Socio-cultural Names of the Manyika

Introduction

Naming is as important as marriage among most of the people of the African continent. The naming practice is a rite of passage that in most cases marks the transition from being in the womb to being a member who is visible and has come into the world of human beings. This explains why among the Manyika like among the other Shona, the death of a child is not really accepted as a big issue. Naming also marks the switch from one status to another, like when one becomes a chief or even a diviner, s/he assumes the name of the founder of the chieftainship or the name of the spirit that would be informing him/her in divination. In the traditional Shona society a child is named in the first week of its birth. A chief is renamed on installation. The names that were given and in some communities are still being given to children relate to meaningful events or circumstances that would have impacted on the family, father or mother of the child during her pregnancy. The names given may also be focusing on events that preceded the period of the pregnancy but had a profound impact on the family or any one of the people who may include the interactions between the woman and her husband's friends. It may be the father who could be naming. He may use that as an opportunity to express his disappointment with his wife or family over certain matters. He may also use the naming opportunity as a platform to express his gratitude to his wife, in-laws and even parents for a good deed that could have been done in the past.

There are other communities where children are initiated into adult life. The best examples for Zimbabwe are those of the Shangani or Tsonga who are found in Masvingo, in Chiredzi and Mwenezi districts that are to the south and south west of the Province respectively and the Remba who are mostly domiciled in the Mberengwa district of the Midlands Province. The Remba who are also known as the vaMwenye are also found in places like Chivi and Gutu in Masvingo Province, Buhera and Nyanga district in Manicaland Province. According to the Mwenye who were discussed with in Nyanga, initiation is no longer as much practiced as it is in Mberengwa. They also confirmed that initiation into adulthood within their group is not accompanied by any change of name. After the initiation the child in the past was given a new name. As has already been discussed above, the same happened when a new chief was installed. At installation, the new chief was and in some communities is still told and advised to leave behind all the other names that he may have been called by and assume a new one, one which in case of chieftainship is the one that was used by the founding father of the dynasty when he founded it.

The Socio-cultural Context of Naming among the Shona in Zimbabwe

In Zimbabwe today, a child may have a minimum of one name and at most in some cases, a maximum of two, although there are cases where children have three or even more names. In situations where children have more than two names, these are usually given as *zita remudumba* (maternity home name), *zita rambuya, sekuru kana imwe hama* (a name given by the grandmother, grandfather [either paternal or maternal] or by any other relative and *zita rerubhabhatidzo* (baptismal name). The maternity home name is usually given within the first week of the birth of the child and in most cases this name is informed by events and other circumstances that could have impacted either positively or negatively on the immediate family. There is also the case of the name by any other relative who may feel that they also have to contribute to the naming ceremony. This of course may be done to avoid clashes over the naming process and so by accepting the other name, the parents of the child will be diffusing tension. The baptismal name is one that is given when a child is christened in the church. This name may be the same that was given in the maternity home although among the Roman Catholics as well as some apostolic sects, a change of name may be required. The purpose of giving a different name in most Christian denominations is predicated on the fact that most Christians believe that baptism itself symbolizes death to the old life (called the life of sin) and resurrecting to a new life that is anchored in spiritualism and righteousness. One who has been baptized is for that reason perceived as a new being and the change in name is also expected to be reflected in word and deed.

From what is given above, it is manifest that names that are given to people, whether they are adults or children, or even names that they give to themselves, are not just attachments. They are products of socio-cultural and at times even of economic processes. This is fundamentally so because in most cases they originate from given socio-economic and cultural settings. They are hardly ever names that are given because the parents or one of the parents feels that it is a beautiful name. In fact, most names that are given among the Shona, whether they are sentential or not, are in most cases responses to particular factors or issues that the one who names would like to bring to the attention of family, friends as well as the community and world at large. The community can become part of the addressee(s) on the same principle that if in Africa it takes a village to raise a child, it then also means that a child or anyone can also be named as a way of addressing the village or community. Even though Jordan (2011: 3) is writing on names of places also called toponyms, what he says equally holds sway for anthroponyms. He states:

Place names are not just attached to certain features of the geographical space, they are not just – colloquially speaking – "hanging around" in space, but they are also attached to a certain social group in the sociological sense, i.e. in the sense of a number of people characterised by mutual relations and a common culture (ranging in size from a family or a couple of friends to a nation). They have in fact been created and are applied by a certain group.

These words, whose focus is on place names as well, go a long way in shedding more light on the societal state of affairs in which even names of human beings are crafted and given.

It is also essential to annotate that the family terrain is a contested space. This is made manifest in the realization that the names that most children finally end having are at times a product of a long process of name negotiation. For example, someone may want to know why a child is being given a particular name. The result is that when someone queries a name s/he may also give another as a suggestion, giving reasons why s/he thinks that to be a better name than the previously suggested. If for example, the mother of a child was the subject of abuse from her husband and his relatives or some of them, she could choose to call her child *Munorwei* (What are you fighting for?/ What is the cause of your fighting me?) This name is in itself a speech act. It is clear that this name is an expression of anger and disappointment or even worry at why the woman would have been treated in the manner that she was. However, the relatives or husband may contest such a name and would possibly dispute it on the basis of the fact that the name is publicizing the family's secrets, which is contrary to what is preached in the Shona proverb *chakafukidza dzimba matenga* (homes are covered by roofs). This proverb means that it does not pay for family members (including daughter-in-law/wives) to announce to the public the problems that they will be facing in their families. This proverb is buttressed by the idiom that is in the imperative clause *usafugure hapwa* (do not open your armpits). Its meaning is the same with that of the proverb that has already been discussed – that one does not have to broadcast to the outsiders problems they will be facing in the home.

A contest may also come about in a situation where for example, the husband's father or mother may want to give the first child of the couple a name. This may cause conflict with both of the young parents feeling that the name has to come from them. They in most cases would argue that they do not want their child or even children named after some persons they do not know about and whom they have never seen. Five young couples that the researcher had discussions with indicated that they were not happy with their in-laws naming their children. They stated that they feared that their children could be named after late ancestors or late relatives who were not of good public standing morally, materially or both. To them therefore, to name children after such people was to invite the spirits of these people to come upon the named children. This, they argued, was likely to be a stumbling block in the children's lives both materially and spiritually. Their main concern was if the person whom the child was named after was for example, a murderer, the belief is that the child is also likely to grow up and become like his/her namesake.

Some among these same couples also added that they considered the act of the in-laws of naming their children as a deed of intrusion and interference within their families. When three grandparents were also asked, they responded by stating that it is their perception as well as according to their tradition, that the naming of a child who will be the first that a new couple would be having was the prerogative of the grandparents. They argued that it was them as the parents of the couple, but especially as the parents of the groom who knew how he had come into being. When asked to clarify this point, they stated that having children or raising children is no easy task. So when a child has grown up to become a family man, it is the best sign of gratitude for him to give his parents the chance to name his first child. The parents further argued that the couple would also have an opportunity to name the first child of their children. So as far as they are concerned, it is not true that the new parents would have been denied a naming opportunity. Their opportunity to name would not only come on subsequent births but also on the first children of their offspring.

There are situations when the conflict may be between in-laws themselves. The husband's parents may opt for a certain name which the bride's parents may consider to be not to their liking. They may suggest their own name. Such conflicts usually come up when the husband's mother's name would have been given to the couple's first child if it so happens that the child is a girl. The bride's mother may also want her name to be given to a particular child since among the Manyika it is considered a great honour to have a child named after you. Cases of the bride's parents interfering in the naming process are few though. The reason possibly lies in the realization on the groom's parents that when a girl-child gets married, she assumes a new identity – that of her husband's family, so to insist on naming a child who traditionally speaking is of the son-in-law is synonymous with declaring that they know another person who may have sired the child. To therefore insist on naming the child is not only considered scandalous but also as the height of stupidity and folly. There are however, situations where the wife's parents may, on the invitation of the husband's parents also give the first child a name. This explains why some children end up having two or three names that is if the parents of the child also insist on having their name considered.

Some of the factors that lead to naming include those that have already been discussed above – those that relate to the typologies and categories that Kahari (1990: 282-3) has discussed. But there are also instances when names come about as a result of observed behaviour patterns. When such names are given to newly born babies, they are considered memory carriers. When they are however given to people who already have names of their own they are called nicknames. Although the term nickname has several possible meanings, for example, shortened versions of names that are also common among the Manyika, they are also descriptive names that bring to the fore the positives or negatives that come out of a particular person. According to Pei (1965: 76) a nickname that is also called an *ekename* is an additional name that is usually bestowed on a person for the purposes of precise identification. This insight is informative in that it makes it clear that names that are given for purposes of identification are largely descriptive for the reason that it is the description that they carry that makes the identification of the named easier. Another interesting aspect about nicknames is that some become permanent while others are transient. In this time and age where physical mobility is high, one can get as many nicknames as possible. Not all of them will remain.

Nicknames may be used to refer to some physical aspects such as height and weight. They may also be used to describe the complexion of a particular person. A good example of such a nickname that the named has come to accept is *Makitikiti* (One who causes the ground to reverberate as he walks). The nickname is derived from the reduplicated ideophone *kiti kiti* that refers to the heavy steps that are usually made by huge beasts, not human beings. According to some informants who were at Avila Mission in the heartland of the Hwesa people between 1976 and 1978 the name was given to one huge bully whose steps could be heard from far off, about thirty to fifty metres away as he went about forcing the physically weak to give him peanut butter. The described person is no longer resident among the Hwesa, but the nickname has stuck with him ever since. The name was also not given to him by the Hwesa, but by the Manyika who were resident among the Hwesa in the Fombe area. These like those at Mhokore and Nyamudeza had been moved to those areas by the Rhodesian regime as it wanted land for the settlement of white immigrants especially after the Second World War (1939-45). Another nickname that is descriptive is *Panhuwadhiziri* (One who is excited by the smell of diesel). The name came about as a result of one acting headmaster in a given school who would always want to ride on a certain diesel truck that had been donated to the Tangwena community in the late 1980s and was in use up to the early 1990s. It is said by some of the informants that on every occasion he heard the sound of the truck, he would abandon whatever work he was doing and create an excuse to join the driver to either Nyanga or Troutbeck which were usually the diver's destinations.

The above discussion has shown how some names come about. They are a result of several factors, among them contests between different but interested parties who would all for example, like to name newly born babies. It has highlighted the reality that naming among the Manyika, along with other Shona groups is largely circumstantial. It is a product of its socio-cultural and even economic environment as the transport operator Masenda's business name *Kurima Kwakanaka* (It is good to be a successful farmer) makes apparently clear. It is said that Masenda, whose bus transport company is now defunct made a lot of money from farming. It is out of this venture that he saved enough that enabled him to launch his business career as a public transport operator.

The next section of the discussion focuses on selected names that are in the socio-cultural realm that includes the economic, but excludes the religious. It attempts to unravel from what the researcher got from informants and also deduced from the names that he heard, and some debates on certain names that he participated in the factors and circumstances that may have led to the giving of these names and other related ones that fall into this category.

Discussion of selected names

Names are an important part of most, if not all human languages, and for most people, especially in Africa where people attach so much significance to anthroponyms. They are not mere labels or attachments. They are furthermore ways of speaking. Because they are means of speaking, they can also be described as statements in miniature. According to Langendock (2001) in Makondo (2009: 28) names as primary anthroponyms fulfil three main functions. These are namely, personal names that are used to address (i.e. talk to), identification (talk about) and a wide range of sub-categorizations as to gender and expressivity (especially combinability with diminutive and argumentative morphemes). This chapter discusses names not only as a means of identification in the sense of pointing out and discussing issues in families, relationships, communities and the country at large. But besides that, as communicative tools, the paper as well discusses how names are used as a platform of talking to others in a given socio-cultural environment. Some of the names identified do discuss gender relations and as well as how some people perceive the girl child.

Commenting on how the Shona name their children Kahari (1990: 281) notes:

The custom of giving proper names to human beings, domestic animals, modern transport and places operates under a system determined by social conditions and the environment. In this respect, Shona names have significance – even if the meaning is lost – and are 'situation tied.'

This observation of Kahari is appropriate principally when names such as *Hamutendi* (You are ungrateful) are analysed. The name *Hamutendi* like almost all Shona sentential names is a complex nominal construction. This means that as a noun it is made up of a noun prefix (np) and a complex noun stem (cns). The name *Hamutendi* is constructed as follows:

Ø- + - *hamutendi*
(np)   (cns)

As already indicated above, **np** stands for noun prefix while **cns** stands for complex noun stem. The complex noun stem can be broken further into more segments as:

ha - + -	*mu* - + -	*tend* - + -	*i*
infixal	subject	verb	terminal
negative	concord	radical	vowel/negative
formative			terminative

So the full constructional pattern is:

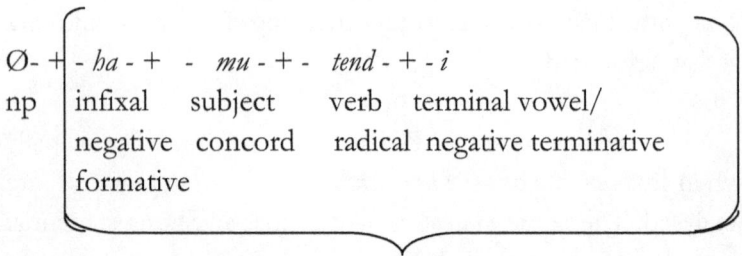

$$\text{Ø-} + \begin{vmatrix} \text{- } ha \text{ - } + & \text{- } mu \text{ - } + \text{- } & tend \text{ - } + \text{ -} i \\ \text{infixal} & \text{subject} & \text{verb} & \text{terminal vowel/} \\ \text{negative} & \text{concord} & \text{radical} & \text{negative terminative} \\ \text{formative} \end{vmatrix}$$

np

(complex nominal stem – cns)

This name is in the expressive category of the speech act theory that was propounded by John Searle, who was expounding Austin's theory. Expressives fall under illocutionary acts, and they are used to express the speaker's attitudes or sentiments such as conveying words of congratulations or thankfulness. They may also be used to express anger and dismay. This is the case that is found in the name *Hamutendi*. This name is an expression of dismay and anger and to some extend frustration. While this discussion is not going to be exhaustive on this name, there is a possibility that one is angry with certain people, whom in the namer's opinion have shown that they are ungrateful. It is essential to comprehend the fact that among the Shona it is expected (and is usually the norm) for family members to help one another especially in cases where an elder brother/sister or a sister/brother-in-law assist the disadvantaged such as brothers and sisters or brothers/sisters-in-law if the parents of these have died or have no financial capacity to look after their children. The assistance normally comes in the form of clothing, feeding as well as sending the disadvantaged to school and in some instances right up to university. These same people can also assist their own in-laws if these are in financial dire straits. When such help is given, it is expected that in the least those who were assisted or are still being assisted would acknowledge the assistance that they will be getting or got. At worst, they do not have to behave or talk in a manner that shows disrespect to those who would have assisted them. It is usually when one feels that s/he is not being appreciated, but has even become an object of ridicule that s/he names a child *Hamutendi*. This confirms what Makondo (2009: 62) observes when he asserts that personal names are used in performative (pragmatic) ways, serving different functions in different social contexts. This is true of the name *Hamutendi*. It is addressing social relations at the family level.

The same name can also be used as a platform for addressing the larger community. It may happen that someone has done a lot in helping his/her community, but for some reasons, most of the members of that neighbourhood do not show that they are grateful. Some may even pour scorn on the philanthropic acts of those who would have come to their assistance and proclaim privately or publicly that they do not have to expect to be thanked because no one would have asked for their help or forced them to give that help. In such a situation word may filter to the concerned people who would have embarked on the philanthropic work and if it so happens that the wife is pregnant, when she delivers the couple may respond by calling their child *Hamutendi*. When a child is thus named, this confirms and upholds Mandende's opinion that:

Africans prefer a name that they can really identify with, a personal name that will always remind them of something in their life experience (2009: 22).

In the case of the name *Hamutendi,* the anthroponyms become a summary statement of how ungrateful some people can be to those who would have helped them. The name may also function as a warning to others who may be interested in giving help that they have to be prepared to be scorned upon by those they would have assisted or their relatives.

As an expressive speech act, this same name is also emotion laden. As an emotional statement, the namer is expressing the feelings that s/he has not been understood and appreciated, and by naming the child thus, s/he is making it clear that s/he has been deeply hurt.

Although the name *Hamutendi* is an expressive speech act, it is also equally a declarative speech act. As a declarative, the name makes an assertion, a statement that some people are ungrateful. This is a complete statement and thus a sentence. The namer is giving this anthroponym because s/he believes in his/her observation that the people s/he helped have not been grateful. Those who are being addressed by this name know how to show their gratefulness.

As both a declarative and an expressive statement, the name may also be given by a wife who feels unappreciated by her husband. She may have started off with her husband when both were not very much materially endowed but these were gained over the years of the subsistence of their matrimony. It may then happen that with the passage of time the husband who may have seen this improvement in their material position an opportunity for him to get a second wife. In the event of such an occurrence, the first wife may name her child *Hamutendi* because to her the husband has chosen to share the family wealth that they both sweated for with an outsider. To this first wife this action by her husband is not just a sign of betrayal but of being ungrateful and as well shows lack of appreciation for the sacrifices that both husband and wife made in an effort to improve their situation.

In the Manyika set-up, like in any other Shona and most Bantu families, a boy child is highly cherished. In life it however does happen that a couple for lack of a better word may become unfortunate and fail to have a boy child. Usually couples are very worried when they have a first, second or third girl (in a time when as many as ten or more children borne of one woman was the norm), the couple would start getting worried. In such a situation, it was believed that there was need to turn the snake (*kupindura nyoka*), which is the use of indigenous medicines in an effort to secure the birth of a boy child since boys were considered important as the family line is believed to continue through the males and not females. If these attempts fail and one continues to have girls only, then it is possible that one can give his next daughter the name *Hazvienzani* (Things [Situations] cannot be the same/ My situation is better). This name which because of its being the first name of a person is in class 1a is constructed as follows:

Ø- + - *hazvienzani*
(np)   s(cns)

The complex noun stem which under other circumstances is a full verbal clause and therefore a verbal sentence can be broken further into more segments as:

ha - + - *zvi* - + - *enzan* - + - *i*
infixal   subject   verb   terminal
negative   concord   radical   vowel/

67

formative   negative
                                             terminative

The full constructional pattern of the word becomes:

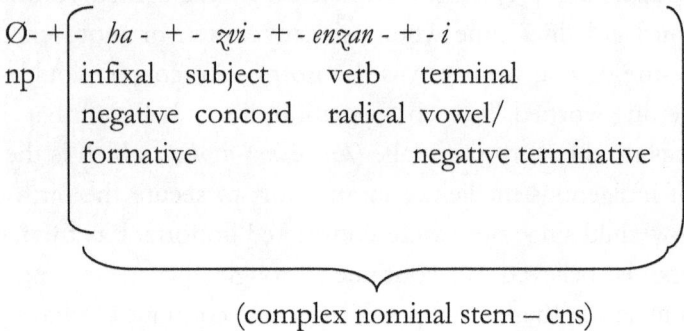

$$\varnothing\text{-} + \begin{array}{l} \text{-} \ ha \text{-} \ + \text{-} \ zvi \text{-} \ + \text{-} \ enzan \text{-} \ + \text{-} \ i \\ \text{np} \quad \text{infixal} \quad \text{subject} \quad \text{verb} \quad \text{terminal} \\ \quad \text{negative} \quad \text{concord} \quad \text{radical} \quad \text{vowel/} \\ \quad \text{formative} \qquad\qquad\qquad\qquad \text{negative terminative} \end{array}$$

(complex nominal stem – cns)

It is important to note that the name *Hazvienzani* is a declarative statement where the namer (most likely the father) is stating that he is actually in a better situation than those who do not have children. This name is also very much in the category of *zita remudumba* (maternity home name) (Kahari 1990: 282) that is given after the people, especially the father, have noted that the child, like others before her is a girl. This name and the father's acceptance of the girl child is not a result of choice but of circumstances beyond his control. When such an occurrence hits one in the face, it is possible to hear the father or other members of the family accepting the situation by stating a proverb like *munhu munhu, haatsikwi ngebweba* (Every person is a human being and s/he can thus not be crushed by a stone) or a related one. This proverb is openly stating that all children, no matter their sex, are human

68

beings and therefore deserve to be accepted and respected as such.

The same name may also be given later in the life of a child. The child who is renamed may be a boy or girl (Shona names are largely unisex) but is the only one of his/her parents, after others have died due to some epidemic, human caused or natural. It may also be because the parents have failed to have other children after this one. When such a situation arises, a child who may at one time have been called *Tafara* (We are happy) may be changed to *Hazvienzani*. In this case the parents are stating to the world that despite their tragic losses or their failure to have another child, they are better than other couples that have no child or have lost all their children to the illness. Mandende's observation best sums up such a naming practice. He notes:

> In traditional African societies there are a number of factors that influence the choice of a personal name. African people are observant of what is happening around them, and they want to record this through personal names (2009: 22).

The name *Hazvienzani,* if the words of Mandende are analysed is one of those cases where a name is being given after people have observed what is happening around them that they do wish to record for posterity. This name like most Shona names captures the people's sentiments. It is a précis of their fears, foibles as well acknowledgement about life's upheavals. Through such names people make known to the world their feelings and the named child becomes a moving and leaving embodiment of either the beautiful or ugly experiences that one would have gone through.

Mapara, Nyota and Mutasa (2011: 11) observe that names are a given as a way of expressing joy, caution, anger, appreciation or any emotion that comes to the fore at the time that a child is born. In the case of the name being examined, it can be realized that it may be given in a grudging appreciation, but more as an expression of an emotion. It may happen that a child who is born is either a cripple or an albino. Such children are normally perceived as a *shamhu* (a whip) that is being used to punish the parents for an offense that they or some unknown ancestors may have committed. When such a name is given, the parents would be saying that it is better to have a cripple or an albino for a child than have no child at all.

Relations at family, clan, community, national or even political levels are not always cordial. There are times when these are mired in controversy and conflict. It is possible that one may feel rejected by family, friends and the community at large. In the political arena, one may also find himself abandoned by allies and supporters. When such an eventuality dawns on the abandoned person, he may end up naming a new child *Hatinawedu/Hatinewedu* (We are all alone/ There is no one for us). This name is constructed as follows:

Ø - + - hatinawedu
np   cns

As can be seen in the example above, this name like *Hazvienzani* is also in noun class 1a.The constructional pattern of the complex stem is as follows:

ha - + - *ti -* + - *na -* + - *wedu*
infixal   subject   auxiliary   possessive (phrase)
negative concord   verb
 formative   radical

The full constructional pattern of the name as observed above has to reflect the fact that it has become not only a personal name but also that it is made up of different morphological constituents. It therefore becomes:

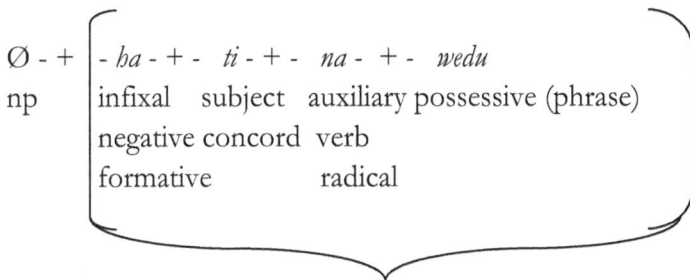

Ø - +   *- ha -* + - *ti -* + - *na -* + - *wedu*
np   infixal   subject   auxiliary possessive (phrase)
         negative concord   verb
         formative   radical

(complex nominal stem – ***cns***)

This name is a summary of the tragedy that has befallen a particular individual. As it is, it is an expression of an emotion – an emotion of anger as well as dejection after the realization that no one is in his camp that is if it is in political circles. At family level the name *Hatinawedu* may equally be an expression of feeling rejected by the husband's family or possibly by that of the wife. The causes of the rejection vary and may remain unknown as well as non-existent. For example, in political circles, both traditional and modern, one may have banked on the support of certain key players who may be in the opinion of the contestants would be kingmakers. When the results of proceedings come out one may then realize that all people or most of the people voted for or sided with the other contestant. It is after such a scenario that one may name a child *Hatinawedu*.

At the family level, one may feel betrayed even by his father's children, including those with whom they have the same mother. It is again important to note that such severing in his eyes of 'blood bonds' may cause him to name his child *Hatinawedu*. In this case the name *Hatinawedu* highlights the fact that despite the fallacies and misrepresentations of most historians such as Beach of the Shona people as always peace-loving and not war-like as the Ngunis, the Ndebele in particular, Shona names do reflect the conflicts that permeate most societies. Although he is writing on Chimurenga names, Pfukwa's observation best sums up what is carried in personal names such as *Hatinawedu*. He states, "As a short text, names are strategies of remembering the beautiful and the ugly in society" (2012: *viii*).

This is very apt of the name that is being analysed here. It is being used by the namer as a platform to express his feeling of betrayal and being unwanted in a community he at one time felt he was part of. The name reflects the ugly side of human relations and the shifting sands on which allegiances are built. Allegiances as the name would always remind the namer, are always constantly shifting and should therefore be looked at with suspicion.

The name *Hatinawedu* may also be given as a response to an invitation to a particular person to come to the support of a given individual. As already noted, this could be at family or political level. May be because of reasons such as being related to both parties, the invitee may opt to remain neutral in the contest between the two sides. He is that type of person who is not worried about who would win between these two. If it so happens that the invitee has a wife who is pregnant and she gives birth, he may give the child who is born the name *Hatinawedu*. In some instances, the name may be given to a grandchild if it happens that s/he is born immediately after such an event. This name becomes a declarative statement where the person who feels let down will be stating publicly that he is comfortable with any one of them coming to the post.

Related to the name *Hatinawedu* is *Hamunakwadi*. While the other names that have been discussed so far are first names, this one has the distinction of being a family name or surname. Surnames among the Shona do not always start as such. They go through an evolutionary process where they start off as either first, even second and third names or nicknames. According to one of the informants who is an uncle to those who bear this name as their family name, the anthroponym *Hamunakwadi* originated as a nickname. It was given to one person of the Shumba (Lion) totem who always felt that people could not be trusted since they could cause havoc in his life. He may have feared that people were out to injure or kill him through whatever means were at their disposal although the fear of being struck by lightning among the Manyika is a reality that causes people to believe that someone can always send lightning to kill them. The other problems that he could have been subtly referring to include witchcraft, or just a feeling of being back-stabbed by colleagues whom one had initially considered as very close, but only to discover that they have abandoned him.

It is significant to note that the word *wadi* in Manyika means the state of being fit, well and health. If people are said to be *wanhu wasiri wadi* or *wasina kwadi* it in Manyika means people who are unwell or people of evil intentions. The context determines what is being meant. The name is therefore an accusatory statement that is clearly making it open that the one who is complaining does not trust some of the people around him/her. Unfortunately in such situations where one is always making such a statement, it is him/her who ends up being called by the statement s/he is always uttering. This is how the name *Hamunakwadi* came into being. Having started off as a nickname describing a particular person, it has become a surname of the descendants of one who bore this nickname. It is a name that carries the memories of a family. Its meaning clearly reflects what Jacobs (1995: 13) observes when he asserts:

> Our names are more than merely identification tags, encoded in them are, above all, our particular life stories, and narratives in which we have our individual being.

These words are quite apt for the name *Hamunakwadi*. The name captures the fears real or imagined of a particular being who has little trust in fellow human beings, especially those who are close to him.

The name *Hamunakwadi* is constructed as follows:

Ø- + - *hamunakwadi*
(np)   (cns)

As is the case with the other names that have been discussed above, the stem of the name *Hamunakwadi* is as follows:

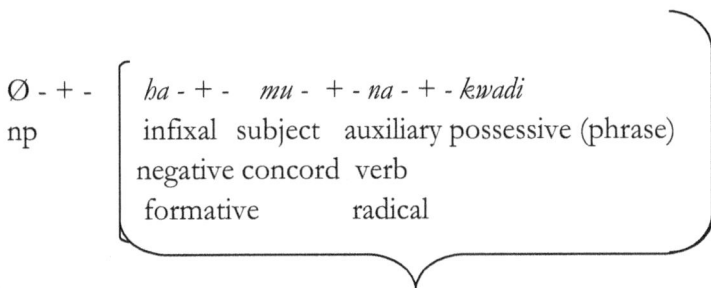

$$\varnothing \text{ - + -} \quad \text{np} \quad \begin{cases} ha \text{ - + -} \quad mu \text{ - + - } na \text{ - + - } kwadi \\ \text{infixal} \quad \text{subject} \quad \text{auxiliary possessive (phrase)} \\ \text{negative concord} \quad \text{verb} \\ \text{formative} \qquad \text{radical} \end{cases}$$

(complex nominal stem – *cns*)

Like the other names that have been thus discussed, this anthroponym also belongs to noun class 1a.

Shona names as part of a living language are found as components of what in linguistics are referred to as pragmatics. According to Cruse (2000: 16 cited in Cummings 2009: 2) pragmatics can be defined as:

> [P]ragmatics can be taken to be concerned with aspects of information (in the widest sense) conveyed through language which (a) are not encoded by generally accepted convention in the linguistic forms used, but which (b) none the less arise naturally out of and depend on the meanings conventionally encoded in the linguistic forms used, taken in conjunction with the context in which the forms are used.

These words are significant in that they do not only capture the main gist of the names that have been discussed above, but also that of the other names that this chapter is continuing to discuss as well as those that will be left out of the discussion due to the issue of space and time. One other such name that falls into this category is *Hamufari* (You are not happy/ You are not pleased), which one of the names that a namer may give to a child. The name *Hamufari* is a mirror of social reality. When people are together, there are those who celebrate the success of others, and there are yet others who fail to appreciate and cherish the happiness and successes of others. It is in situations such where people do not only fail to express happiness but on the contrary display disgust and hate that lead to such a name being given to a newly borne baby. It is possible that the name may be given by a wife to her newly borne child because she may have a feeling that she is not wanted not only by her husband but also by her husband's relatives, especially her in-laws. This is worsened in a set-up where the husband's family openly supports their son getting a second or more wives. When a situation similar to the one described above arises, the name itself becomes an elliptical sentence that in full can be rendered as *Hamufari nekuva kwangu pano* which as a proper noun will be written as one word thus: *Hamufarinekuvakwangupano* (You are not happy with my presence in this homestead or in this family).

Another situation that may lead to the giving of the name *Hamufari* may emanate from the realization on the part of a couple that they have been blessed by a baby girl, but the baby is not welcome in other circles especially by the husband's parents who would have been expecting a baby boy whom to them is a *mudyi wenhaka* (the heir). Because they already expect the flak they are going to receive from the husband's parents, some friends and relatives, they may also settle for the name *Hamufari*. This name is given with the intention of pre-emptying any criticism that may come their way. In this case, the child becomes the conduit through which the parents are stating that they know the people's expectations, but these could not be fulfilled hence the name. The parents are in a way saying that they are aware people are not happy with their new baby who is a girl, but they cannot do anything since that is beyond their control.

As noted in the foregoing paragraph, while human relations may not be as rosy as experiences reflect, among the Manyika, the birth of a son like among other Shona groups is received with joy. The act of procreation itself is in some instances perceived as a contest between the husband and wife. If a wife gives birth to a baby girl, this in most families is frowned upon. They however hope that the next pregnancy will see the birth of a son. When a baby boy is born to a couple that has been praying for it especially for a very long time, the son may be given the name *Takunda* (We have overcome). This name clearly points out the reality of the contest that would be between the two sexes in their home. Another name that may be given is *Tamuka* (We are revived). This name implies that the state of having girls only in a family is just as good as marking the death of that particular lineage. When the name *Tamuka* is given it is therefore an expression of joy that finally the lineage that was feared to be getting into oblivion is now revived.

Given the fact that names are speech acts, it is important to note that as speech acts; their being given is equivalent to some form of action. According to Campsall[12] the speech act theory attempts to explain human utterances as having three parts or aspects, namely: locutionary, illocutionary and

[12] www.universalteacher.org/uk/language/prgamatics.htm

perlocutionary. These have already been discussed in chapter one, but here the writer would again like to re-focus on the perlocutionary aspect or act. The effect of the perlocutionary act on the listener(s) is such that they cause him or her to accept for example, a pledge, bet or any statement. The perlocuctionary act also evokes the state of acceptance that is evoked by the use of the name *Kufa* (To die/Death). The name *Kufa* is given by those who would have lost dear ones or several children in succession. Through this name they will be declaring that death has become so common place in their lives that they choose to name a new child under the influence of this phenomenon. They may also give the name as a way of expressing their anguish at how death would have robbed them of their loved ones.

It is also important to note that among the Manyika when a person dies, some elders do not mourn as much as the younger ones. This has often created problems with the younger ones accusing the elderly of witchcraft. What the younger ones fail to comprehend in most cases is that this is not a sign that the elders do not care or that they dabble in acts of witchcraft. Their actions are only an indication that they come to accept that death despite the fear and suffering it brings into people's lives – is a reality and a certainty. They have come to accept and appreciate the fact that no matter how rich or poor a person is, it will always come. This explains why at times one would hear an elderly person utter the words, *"Rwake apedza. Rwasarira isu"* (S/he has completed her/his task or journey. The turn is now left to us).This statement is a philosophical way of coping with death, but it at the same time confirms the reality of death as part of humanity. The point the elders would be making is that everyone who is living will one day die, it may be sooner or later, but death is the definite grim reaper. The acceptance of death as reality is as well captured in the saying, *"Hapana asingafi"* (There is no one who does not die). It is this reality that the Manyika like the other Shona groups have also immortalized through names such as *Kufa* which is either the first part of a full name or the second part of the same full name, depending on the namer of course. It may also be a case of a name that is open-ended, where people choose to fill the last part of the name as they wish. Another name that functions in a similar fashion with this one is *Hakutizwi* (It/That place cannot be run away from).

The name *Kufa* is a shortened version of a name that in typical Shona fashion is open-ended. As has already been stated in the preceding paragraph, this name is that type of anthroponym that gives one room to add what s/he thinks best suits a situation. While the name is a summary of events that relate to death and the acceptance of the inevitability of it, when used in different contexts, the name can be rendered as either *Kufahakutizwi* (Death cannot be run away from/ No one escapes the jaws of death) or *Kufahakunashasha* (Death does not spare even champions). The first version is normally used when an ordinary person dies. The second version is on the other hand used when a person who is rich, famous or even notorious dies. Even though it is generally not accepted that people celebrate the death of a fellow human being, when the second version of this name is used, there is some element of subtle celebration over a given death. This however, depends on how the now late person would have related to the others when s/he was alive. If one was arrogant, proud and cruel, then it is clear such a name would be given to a child of those who would have been victims of their arrogance or whatever vice the affected would have

79

perceived. The second version is today also rendered as *Kufahakunamemba* (Death reaches even those who are in high class or those who make pretensions at being high class).

This name is made up of two major constituents namely the subject, which is *Kufa* (To die/ Death) and the predicate *hakutizwi/hakuna shasha* (one cannot run away from it/ does not spare champions). Its use in grammatical terms is a case of gerunding, a situation where an infinitive verb is used to function as a noun. Chalker and Weiner (1994: 171) note that this term (gerunding) is falling out of common use stating:

> Both the term *gerund*, from Latin grammar, and the term *verbal noun* are out of favour among some grammarians, because nounlike and verblike uses of the – *ing* form exist on a cline. For example, in *My smoking twenty cigarettes a day annoys them, smoking* is nounlike in having a determiner (*my*), and in being the head of the phrase (*my smoking twenty cigarettes a day*), which is the subject of the sentence; but it is verblike in taking an object and adverbial (*twenty cigarettes a day*), and it retains verbal meaning.

Even though these two, Chalker and Weiner (1994) state that the term *gerunding* is falling out of favour with grammarians, the example that they give is relevant when it is applied to some Shona names. Barring the fact that the term *gerund* is said to be falling out of favour with grammarians, in Shona the practice of *gerunding* is very common especially when one looks at the noun classification system of the language. In Shona all class 15 nouns are verbal nouns. They are verbal in nature but they play the role of nouns. So the name *Kufahakutizwi* when not used as a first name can be written as a statement like: *Kufa hakutizwi* (Death cannot be run away from) where *kufa* is the subject and *hakutizwi* is the predicate (an inflected verb phrase). These names help the reader to also understand the Shona worldview. They believe and accept that human life at least for an individual in his or her physical form does not go on forever but comes to an end through death. This is even immortalised by the late Shona poet, Wilson Benedict Chivaura in his poem "Kutya Kurova" (Fear of permanently coming to an end [1996: 33]).

Commenting on the importance of context in a communicative event, but with a special focus on pragmatics, Cummings (2009: 4) observes:

> No definition of pragmatics would be complete in the absence of some mention of context. The notion of context extends beyond its obvious manifestation as the physical setting within which an utterance is produced to include linguistic, social and epimistic factors.

These words are essential in the understanding of the Shona naming practices. As has already been mentioned in the early pages of this book and foregoing chapters, naming is a form of communication and the context within which a child is born also determines the name that that child will get, besides how each birth will be used as a communication platform. This point is additionally illuminated in the way some people in Chief Tangwena's area named their children at the height of Rhodesian settler rule. For the Tangwena people, the coming of white settlers was a curse that they chose to resist. One of the ways of resisting was by refusing to move away from the ancestral lands.

There is need to here put the picture of what was prevailing in perspective. The taking away of the Blacks' land was based on the White settlers' wrong assumption that the land was unoccupied. This is made very distinct by the representative of white settler rule in Zimbabwe Ian Douglas Smith who says that when the Pioneer Column came, they had a clear conscience because as far as they were concerned the area was unoccupied. He states that the Ndebele had moved into unoccupied territory with the only inhabitants being "wandering Bushmen" (Smith 2007: 1). He further states:

> The eastern parts of the country were settled by a number of different tribes, nomadic people who had immigrated from the north and east, constantly moving to and fro in order to accommodate their needs and wants (*ibid*).

These words are very pertinent in that they are a window through which Rhodesian thoughts on the land issue were perceived. They saw the whole land as largely unoccupied and to them it was meant for their taking. This was the lie that had to give to the world in an effort to justify their occupation of the land as well as its sequestration from its original inhabitants. Blacks were non-existent in as far as the land question was concerned. It is with such arrogance and impunity that they approached the Tangwena land issue.

In 1964, at what they called the Gaeresi Ranch, the Rhodesian Front authorities tried to evict the Tangwena people and their chief Rekayi from their ancestral homeland. This land in the Nyanga Mountains is rich agricultural land that some of the white settlers called 'New England' because of its weather. They really loved it, and not surprisingly 250 000 acres of it was 'sold' in 1905 (without the knowledge of the inhabitants) by the BSAC to the Anglo-French Matabeleland Company. This Anglo-French Matabeleland Company latter ceded part of this land to the Gaeresi Ranch Company. As is the case with the way the whites dealt with blacks, the Tangwena were not made aware of this alienation of their land until 1965, when the manager of the ranch decided in the interests of economic farming to extend his fencing to encompass them. This decision of the ranch manager coincided with the death of the former Tangwena chief and the election of Rekayi as his successor. The intention of the white farmer was to 'rationalize' by reducing the African population now included, and offered labour contracts to some Tangwena, expecting the rest to move to whichever 'reserve' the District Commissioner prescribed. Here, however, something that had never transpired somewhere else where blacks had lost their lands happened: Rekayi Magodo Tangwena and his people refused to move. Austin who writes about the apartheid system that was practiced in Rhodesia observes that many Africans have protested at similar moves, but none with such dignity and determination (1975: 32).

Their refusal had serious repercussions for the evictees. Besides losing their livestock, some of them also lost their children to the Rhodesian authorities who took them away as punishment and initially kept them in holding camps under the Department of Social Welfare. The total number of children that the Rhodesian authorities took away as a punishment on the Tangwena people and as a way of forcing them out is really not known but according to some sources it was about a hundred or so youngsters[13]; Austin 1975: 32-3). These children were later handed over to mission stations such as Triashill and St Barbara's in Mutasa District, Makumbi Visitation in Chinamhora and Arthur Shirley Cripps Children's Home at St John's Chikwaka in Goromonzi.

Besides resisting physically, the Tangwena people also responded to the white menace through the names that they gave to their children. The names that they gave during this time reflect their predicament. They tell the story of a people who at times are at a loss on what to do or in some instances who ask questions that reflect their anger at the white settler regime and its unyieldingness that was fired more by racial superiority than by issues of justice. The names reflect the predicament of a people who found themselves being victims of a government that made decisions on purely racial grounds instead of being a government for all the people. These same names are indicators of the Tangwena people's awareness of themselves as a people. Some of the children who were born during this time bear names such as *Takaedza*, *Toitasei* and *Togarasei*.

The person called *Takaedza* (We tried our best [to kick out the whites]) passed away in the late 1980s. According to his father, one Lazarus Nyakurita, who was one of the informants, the name was given to his first son as a statement expressing disappointment with the fight against the settlers who had come into the Tangwena area. It is a statement of surrender and despair. *Takaedza* his first son was born around 1966/67 and this was at the beginning of the clashes between the Tangwena people and the Smith regime. By giving his son

---

[13] http://hansard.millbanksystems.com/lords/1972/aug/04/rhodesia-future-of-tangwena-children

this name, the father was departing from the norm, where people gave names to their children after being informed by family and community events. While according to him the name was addressing the problems that the Tangwena people were facing as a result settlerism, it was also addressing a bigger political problem that the blacks in colonial Zimbabwe were facing. Most blacks had been kicked off their lands. It is also important to note that the name *Takaedza* was also given by one who on the surface appears to be giving up or has already given up the fight against settler land grabbing practices. The fight in this case is against the white farmer, who is supported by the Ian Smith regime that had declared independence unilaterally from the United Kingdom on 11 November 1965.

Morphologically, the name *Takaedza* is constructed as follows:

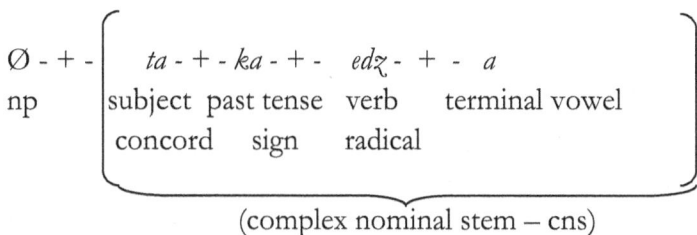

$$\varnothing - + - \overbrace{\begin{array}{llll} ta - + - ka - + - & ed\underline{z} - + - & a \\ \text{subject} \quad \text{past tense} & \text{verb} & \text{terminal vowel} \\ \text{concord} \quad \text{sign} & \text{radical} \end{array}}$$

np

(complex nominal stem – cns)

This name is making a public announcement that the Tangwena people had made an effort to remain on their land through dialoguing with the new claimant to their homeland but this was to no avail. As has already been pointed out above, the other message that is carried out in the name is that they had tried but the outcome of their effort was disappointment.

Another name, that one Langton Mabvudza gave to his first and eldest son is *Toitasei* (What shall we do?) This name is made up of two words, *toita* and *sei* which combine to form the question *Toita sei?* (What shall we do? or What is to be done?) The question is being asked as a response to the menace of Rhodesian settlersim which was threatening their livelihoods. The Tangwena had no military means of fighting the Smith regime, so they were left to ask the question, *Toita sei* (What shall we do?) in the face of this monster? The name that this man gave to his son highpoints the dilemma that the Tangwena people were facing as a consequence of being forced off their land by an outsider, one who claimed to have bought their land from a company, and yet the existence of that company was not even known to the Tangwena people. Such was the evil nature of colonialism that European companies parcelled the lands of the blacks among themselves without even considering the indigenous inhabitants. The value of this name in bringing to the fore the plight of the Tangwena people is amplified by Finnegan (2012: 455) who notes that names among Africans often play an indispensable part in oral literature. As part of oral literature they comment on the prevailing situation so they become part not only of a living culture but also of a living literature and heritage. She states some of the value of the names by stating, "Names can be used as a succinct and oblique way of commenting on their owners or on others" (Finnegan 2012: 456).

Langton Mabvudza had another son born after 1972 when the Smith regime took away some Tangwena children who were housed at Nyafaru. These children as already stated above were initially under the custody of the Department of

Social Welfare, and were later handed over to mission stations for them to look after. It is after this incident that he named his newly born son *Togarasei?* (How shall we live?) This name as a speech act expresses anger and disappointment at the way the Tangwena people were being treated by a government that claimed that it had the world's happiest blacks and that they were treated as equals (Smith 2007: 107, 375, 408). This of course was an untruth because it is quite contrary to what the Ian Smith regime subjected the Tangwena people to. How could they be happy when they were dispossessed? May be Smith meant the most passive of blacks, but happiest? That is not true. The Tangwena people did not only lose their children. Their homes were moreover burnt down and in addition their livestock was taken by the Rhodesian government. The name *Togarasei* is therefore very befitting because it shows the callousness of the Smith regime that claimed to be waging a war against communists and promoting the Christian Western civilisation when in actual fact it was behaving like the Nazis and fascists whom ironically Smith strongly condemns in his autobiography (Smith 2007: 65, 147, 187). The Tangwena people were not a happy people. They were a harassed lot that endured the wrath of a racist regime that did not brook any opposition and resistance to its machinations. It was therefore appropriate to ask: *Togara sei?*, by giving the name *Taogarasei*

Conclusion

This chapter has discussed the social and cultural forces that inform people in their naming practices. It has noted that relations at both family and community level do inform the namers as they choose names for the newly born or when they change names to reflect their new status. Some of the names that people give to their newly born babies are at times a response to what the community would have said to either the father or mother of the newly born child. This has been exemplified in names such as *Hazvienzani,* where someone is stating that having a girl child is better than being childless. The political environment also has a very significant role to play in the names that parents give to their children. While the necessities of a guerrilla warfare may cause someone to give him/herself a *nom de guerre,* those involved at a local level or as the public face of a guerrilla movement may not use such names. They may however, give their children names that reflect the political situation. What this chapter has also shown is that naming besides not being an arbitrary act, may also be a process of negotiation and such negotiations may at the end leave a child with more than one name. The decision at the end to have all these names or some of them registered with the birth and death registration office depends not only on the parents of the child but also on the pressure brought to bear on the parents of the new baby by the interested parties. In most cases, those who do not put much pressure have their names left out in the registration documents.

Chapter IV

Some Shona Theophoric Sentential Anthroponyms

Introduction

It is generally accepted that Africans are a highly religious people. While not all of them are Christians, some have embraced Christianity as a faith and have syncretised this with their own indigenous African religions. The names that they give to their children and those that they even have for some places are termed theophoric names. The phrase 'theophoric names' is used to refer to names that embed the name of a god, both invoking and displaying the protection of that deity. Those who name will be appreciating the fact that their gods or Supreme Being will not only be protecting them but also showering them with an abundance of blessings. The tragedy with the Shona just like most colonised people everywhere was that most were forcibly converted to Christianity. Although most were not interested in converting to this new religion, they were really left with no option if they wanted to access education which in most cases was provided by missionaries (Zvogbo 1985: 26, Kadhani and Riddel 1981: 60). When one converted to this new religion, s/he was expected to change his or her name as an indication that s/he had died to the old life and resurrected in the new, just like Jesus Christ died and rose on the third day. It is important to note here that the change of name came about after baptism, a ritual that saw a person being immersed in water three times, or had water poured on his head three times with each time being counted as each of the days that Jesus Christ was dead and only rose on the third day. After this act, the baptised person was expected to assume a new name. The name was not to be any name, but had to be a 'Christian' one or one of Eurocentric origin. No African name was accepted as Christian. They were all considered to be pagan and therefore not suitable enough for a 'new' being to use. Chitando (2001: 144) makes this clear when he states:

> In the encounter between western missionaries as propagators of the Christian gospel and African converts, the cultural significance of indigenous names inevitably surfaced. To a very large extent, traditional and culture-bound names were rejected in favor of European, biblical, or "Christian" names.

The major denominations that were culprits in this area were the Catholic churches, both Roman Catholic and Anglican. Even when they got to a place and set up a mission station, it was very rare that they would name the station after the local chief or headman as is the case of Berejena in Masvingo, Zimbabwe. This name is more of an exception rather than the norm because mission stations always got names of saints or martyrs, for example St Patricks and Silveira Mission. Silveira is named after Gonzalo da Silveira, the first European Christain martyr in Munhumutapa's empire. The Dutch Reformed Church is one of the few together with the United Methodist Church that did not compel converts to use names of saints or religious movement leaders. Zimbabwe as a country has also witnessed the mushrooming of Pentecostal Churches. While these ones accept indigenous names, some of the members of these denominations give their children names that are biblical such as Jedaiah, Shemaiah, and Shaddai (Chitando 2001: 150). Such names are however not as prevalent as those in Shona. Unlike the missionary names that most of the people were given during the colonial period, and whose meanings most did not know, the names that most Christians of today give to their children carry their prayers to their Supreme Being. It is these names that are called theophoric names.

Joseph in Pfukwa (2007: 135) best sums up the issue of religious names and their function, stating:

> Ethnic and religious identities concern where we come from and where we are going – our entire existence, not just the moment to moment. It is these identities above that, for most people, give profound meaning to the 'names' we identify ourselves by, both as individuals and as groups.

Although the words above focus on both ethnic and religious names, their significance lies in the fact that they point out the fact that names are pointers to the past as much as they are signposts into the future. The theophoric names that are discussed in this chapter are an avenue into what naming patterns were like under colonial rule as well as the evolution that has occurred with the advent initially of Black Nationalism in the 1960s and the attainment of independence in Zimbabwe in 1980.

Reflections of faith through names

The names that are discussed in this chapter are those of people who are found in Nyanga district's Nyamaropa and

Tangwena areas. The Nyamaropa area, unlike most areas in Zimbabwe has an Irrigation Scheme. The establishment of this scheme in the 1950s saw people from diverse backgrounds as well as from different districts of the province and religious persuasions converging in this area with the interest of venturing into small scale commercial agriculture. Some of the denominations that moved in and have a heavy presence, besides the Roman Catholics who have a mission station nearby called Regina Coeli, are the Anglicans and the United Methodist Church. The Tangwena area has as well of late witnessed the mushrooming of Pentecostal movements that are rivalling the long established Johane Marange Apostolic sect. The coming of these religious movements to both areas has also come with it the abandonment of the use of the so-called 'Christian' names, with people giving their children names from the bible, or Shona names that they believe reflect their faith.

The Shona, since time immemorial have always held their Supreme Being in awe and respect. This fact is reflected not only in the names that they carried but also that they gave to places. What is today called *Matopos* was called *Matombo* (Stones/Rocks). Within these mountains was a cave that the Shona (Rozvi) called *Mwarindidzimu* (God is the Spirit). This place name shows that they worshipped their God, and it is in this cave that they believed God's voice could be heard. Another place that carries a theophoric name is *Munwewamwari* (Finger of God). Although this toponym is descriptive in that it gives a graphic representation of how the mountain looks like, in its very name it also carries the Shona's fear and respect for the Supreme Being. They see the mountain like the finger of God that is pointing up to his heavenly abode. It is also believed that the heavens cannot be pointed at, and so whoever created that mountain are omnipotent and the only being that is like this is *Musikavanhu* (The Creator of Humanity). He is therefore the only one who can point at the heavens.

Theophoric names in the colonial period

While some denominations insisted that new converts were supposed to bear the names of saints, there are others that gave their converts space to name their children in a manner that was not provocative but promoted Christian brotherhood. Among the names that these people gave to their children were anglicised versions of Shona names. Examples of such names are Blessed (*Takomborerwa*) and Blessings (*Zvikomborero/Makomborero*). Although these two names which are versions of the same do not bear the name god in them, they are theophoric because according to the beliefs of the Shona, all blessings come from God, even if it is through a medium or other means.

Colonialism came with it the burden of the migrant labour system. This saw a lot of people moving from rural to urban areas in search of work. However, not all people who went to stay in the urban areas did so because they were looking for employment. Some, especially young men went to the urban areas to escape from girls who would have eloped to them after they had impregnated them. When a child was born and the father would not have acknowledged paternity, but the woman would be convinced of his responsibility in the case, she could name the newly born baby Godknows instead of the Shona version *Mwarianoziva*. This type of name fits in well with the definition of a theophoric name that is given by Haber (2001: 56). He states:

According to the Greek English Lexicon, the meaning of the Greek word "theophoros" is "bearing or carrying a god"; theophoric "nomata" are "names derived from a god." In our discussion here about theophoric names in the Bible, we allude to names built using the two Hebrew denominations of God: Elohim and the Tetragrammaton (hereafter, "the Lord" in our translation). Neither is taken fully, with all their letters, in the building of a biblical theophoric name.

Although Haber is focusing on biblical names, the idea of a name that carries or bears a god is very obvious in most Shona names. They may or may not carry in them the full name of God, but the sense of god or a deity is embedded in the very name itself. The name Godknows is an example of a name that carries God's name in full. When one gives a child such a name after being jilted by a lover, she will be invoking the wrath of God to visit upon the irresponsible lover. It in fact is a curse that has to be borne by the young man. The name can also function as a silent prayer to the Supreme Being to look not only after the child but to empower the mother so that she can fend for her child. This second possible meaning of the name makes it clearly a theophoric name as defined by *Wikipedia* when it observes that a theophoric name is a term that is taken from Greek: θεοφόρητος – *theoforētos*, which means "bearing a deity", entrenches the name of a god, both invoking and displaying the protection of that deity. This definition is in tandem with the silent prayer that is carried in the name Godknows, where the mother is invoking her deity to come to her assistance by punishing her lover who has jilted her.

Another name that was prevalent in the colonial days, especially in the days of the liberation struggle in Zimbabwe is Praise. It also rendered as Praisegod. In Shona this name is *Rumbidzai* and *Rumbidzaishe* or *Rumbidzaimwari*. From a speech act perspective the name Praisegod is a directive. As a speech act it is urging and instructing people to pray to the Supreme Being. To the Shona, including the Manyika, the Creator of the universe is one so even though the term *Mwari* (God) is spelt with a lower case 'm' that does not diminish his importance. It is only spelt thus because of orthographic requirements. This same name may in addition be a constantive. According to Devitt and Hanley (2003)[14] constatives can be used in differing areas such as affirming, alleging, announcing, answering, and attributing. It is also possible to use them for claiming, classifying, concurring, confirming, conjecturing, denying, disagreeing, disclosing, disputing, identifying, informing, insisting, predicting, ranking, reporting and stating as well as stipulating. In the name Praisegod one could be performing any one of the areas identified. For example, because one would have been successful in doing something, he may give credit to his Creator for his success. By naming the child he will be affirming as well as announcing the supremacy of his Creator.

Godgiven (*Tapiwanashe* or *Tapuwanashe*) is a name that parents give to their child as a way of acknowledging that child as a divine present. Such a name may be given after people have struggled to have a child. Some people may want to claim that they are the ones who played a significant role in ensuring that the couple has a child. When the couple that has been so blessed gives their child such a name they are giving credit not to any human being, but to their Creator.

---

[14] http://userwww.sfsu.edu/kbach/Spch.Prag.htm

The use of such names shows that the Shona people's understanding of the Supreme Being is something that they accept as part and parcel of their everyday life. Whether the names are in English or Shona, they reflect the idea of a Supreme Being who is not remote but one who is omnipresent.

Nationalism also brought with it a new consciousness among most of the blacks of Zimbabwe. While some nationalists were giving their children indigenous names, certain Christians also shifted from giving anglicised names to Shona ones. This shift was quite revolutionary because it in a way debunked the missionary myth that there was nothing Christian about Shona names. This period of reawakening seems to have continued to gather steam up to this day, because this researcher has observed that most young Christian families give their children theophoric names. It is to these names that the next section turns to.

Some Shona Christian Sentential Names

The Christian Church in Zimbabwe has undergone a lot of positive change. For instance, in the 1950s, prayers in the Roman Catholic Church were done in Latin. All this changed following the Vatican II Council of 1963-65. African songs and musical instruments were now permitted as means of worship. While the churches were beginning to be more accommodating, changes at the political front also had an impact on how black Christians named their children. They gave their children names that carried meanings that they easily understood and related to. In fact, according to Chitando the change in such naming patterns came about as a result of the attainment of independence in Zimbabwe in 1980. He notes:

> By giving their children names that are charged with Christian theological overtones, Zimbabwean Christians are basically claiming Christianity for themselves. They have made Christianity "a vernacular religion lived through hearing the Word of God 'in our own language'." (2001: 149).

The above words indicate that the names that some the Shona give now to their children reflect that the terrain of naming within the Christian movement is itself a contested space. By giving these names the Manyika, just like the other Shona groups are creating as well as recreating their own space within the Christian church. It is no longer a foreign religion but one that is part and parcel of their lives. This appropriation and acceptance of the western type of Christianity (that Chitando has noted) among the Shona (and other Zimbabweans) has seen some of them especially the young couples giving their children theophoric names. These names are given as ways of expressing gratitude to the Creator for their successes in life or as silent prayers to the Supreme Being to guide them in their life. Unlike the names that have been discussed before, these names are not all necessarily very Manyika because of the interactions between the Manyika and other groups. They are however discussed because they are now also found among the Manyika.

The Manyika, like the other Shona believe in the inevitability of death. While they do not believe in the religious doctrine that subscribes to the idea of hell, they do believe that there is heaven. Because of this acceptance of death as well as the belief in heaven, some Manyika, especially the elderly ones have given their children names such as *Hakutizwikudenga* (The heavens cannot be run away from). Even though in a social context the name may reflect the fact that people have resigned to fate because death is always there, from a religious perspective, the name confirms what the Manyika, like the other Shona groups believe in – that death is what God wishes to occur to his creations and each person has a day that is set for his or her death. This is best explained by the song *"Kwasara kunesu"* (It is our turn that is left), that is sung when people go to bury someone. Elders are at times even heard saying, *"Rwake apedza, zvasarira isu"* (S/he has done her/his part, it is now left to us to also play our part). It is this belief that informs such names.

Besides names such as the one discussed above that focuses on death and the Manyika's acceptance of death some names reflect the fact that it is not all gloom and doom for some people. The Shona are always taught to be grateful for whatever they receive or have. The importance of this appreciation is summed up in the proverb *Chidiki chaunacho tenda kumidzimu yako* (Whatever little that you have, be grateful and thank your ancestors for it). It is possibly with this teaching in mind that the Manyika have also given their children names that bear this message of thankfulness to their Creator. Some of the names that they give thanks are *Tendai* (Give thanks/ Be grateful), *Tatenda* (We are grateful/ Thank you) and *Tinotenda* (We are grateful/ Thank you). Even though these names do not have *ishe* (Lord) at the end this trend is common among, in families that have joined Pentecostal churches the only thanks that can be given are given to the Creator. The reasons for being grateful are varied. Some would like to thank their Creator for giving them a child. This is very important since most Manyika believe that *mwana chipo chinobva kuna Mwari* (a child is a gift that comes from God). Any one of these names may also be given by a couple that would be giving thanks to the Creator for having made them find one another. It is as well possible that one partner may choose any one such name again as a way of expressing gratitude that s/he got a good partner. It is of significance to point out here that the Manyika do not use the term *ishe* (chief) for Lord but use *mambo* (king) which the white colonialists mistranslated as chief. It is also possible that the whites deliberately translated it thus to buttress their argument that blacks had no empires and kingdoms but had small chiefdoms (Beach 1980). The use of the noun *ishe* in Manyika names therefore shows the spread of indigenous Christian movements.

Among the Shona children are very important. Even if a person especially a woman is not married, it is possible to hear some of her friends advising her to at least have her own child even if she has failed to get a partner to marry. In some marriages some couples may struggle to get a child. When they finally get one, it is then possible that a child may be called *Tatenda* or *Tinotenda*. The name in this case is a living reminder that they should always be grateful to their God who has made it possible for them to have a child. Agyekum (2006: 222) highlights the significance of the supernatural in giving children names when he observes that among the Akan there are certain names that they give to children which depict the Akans' belief in the supernatural beings and their power to provide children. He further notes that these names are normally given when parents have struggled for children for a number of years and all hopes are lost. This act of naming a child as a way of giving thanks to the Creator is not peculiar to the Akan. It is also not new to the Shona Christians. Even the Jews of old did that. Haber (2001: 57) makes this clear when he notes that it is an analogous thought that moved Leah, the wife of Jacob, to call her fourth son by the name Yehudah. This name merges the first three letters of the Tetragrammaton with a derivative of *y-d-h* – (thank), of which the first letter became a "*vav*" and merged with the "*vav*" of the Tetragrammaton. He further asserts that Leah herself explained the meaning of this name when she stated, 'Now I will thank the Lord'; therefore she gave him the name Yehudah (Gen. 29: 35). The names *Tinotenda* and *Tatenda* are therefore not different from the Jewish name Yehudah, neither are the Shona the only ones who give theophoric names to their deity.

Some people besides giving thanks to their Creator also believe that whatever success and other positive aspects of life that they will be getting are not by chance but are with heavenly blessings. They therefore attribute their success/es to their Creator. They give their children names that reflect this gratefulness by declaring that they are their Creator's beloved. Instead of giving their child a name such as David, which means 'beloved'[15] they may give their child a Shona name which is also unisex. An example of such a name is *Tadiwanashe* (we are the beloved of the Lord). This name is a declarative statement. The namers are declaring to the public that they are their Lord's beloved and favoured ones. The name of the child is therefore a public confession of faith by the parents. This name also reflects the fact that when parents name a child thus, they are also offering a silent prayer that their God will continue to look upon them with favour. This

---

[15] http://www.behindthename.com/name/david

name falls into the category of what Stuhlman (2004: 14) calls "Names which express hope for the future or a desired condition" for the parents of the child hope that their God would continue to abide by them. Other names that fall within the same category with *Tadiwanashe* are *Isheanotida* (The Lord loves us) and the variant one *Isheanesu* (also given as *Anotidaishe*) which is the equivalent of the biblical Emmanuel which means "the Lord is with us."

Boasts are part and parcel of the Shona way of life. These are normally by a farmer or blacksmith who would have been successful (Mapanje and White 1983: 15) and he would be praising himself. They earlier on state, "In many societies it is common for individuals to praise themselves, summing up their own personality and achievements" (1983: 7). Boasts may also manifest themselves in a subtle way through names. A good example of a name that may be considered as a subtle boast is *Takudzwanashe* (We have been respected by the Lord) which really means "We have found favour in the eyes of the Lord". Although on the surface the name appears to mean that the namer(s) has been favoured by the Lord, it is also a subtle boast where the namer is making a claim to the other believers as well as non-believers that s/he is the favoured one of her or his deity. Another name which though acknowledging that the Lord has favoured him/her is also a boast is *Tafadzwanashe* (The Lord has made us happy). This name like the *Takudzwanashe* has the namer placing her or himself at a higher plane where s/he perceives her/himself as the Lord's favourite. Since this is a name that the converted is giving to his/her child it is possible that the boast could becoming as a result of what one may have read in the bible with special reference to children. The biblical book that is likely to have informed such parents (that is if they are aware of this) is Psalms. In this book it is stated, "Lo, children are a heritage of the LORD, the fruit of the womb is his reward. Like arrows in the hand of a warrior are the sons of one's youth" (Ps. 127: 3, 4). The same book goes on to conclude by saying, "Happy is the man who has his quiver full of them! He shall not be ashamed when he speaks with his enemies in the gate" (vs. 5). Even though the book of Psalms celebrates children, the book of Proverbs goes on to counsel that children can also be the source of grief, even though it as well makes the observation that there is also much joy associated with children (Prov. 3: 1-4).

Some names are open declaratives that carry undertones of boasting. One name that was given was said to be of one who once stayed in the Tangwena area is *Mukundindishe* (The Lord is the victor). By giving a child this name, the parents are declaring to their enemies, real or perceived that they do not fear anyone or any force since the real victor in all matters relating to life is the Lord. The parents may also be boasting, bringing to the attention of other people that their success in life is not really based on their intelligence and wisdom but it comes as a result of their deity's intervention.

It is a common belief among most Manyika that whatever good fortune or misfortune that comes one's way they always believe that the Heavens would have provided that. It is however in situations where parents are in most cases not happy with the gender of the child, or the child that is born to them may have certain disabilities that may be difficult for them to accept. When some elders see such a situation, it is possible that they may intervene and give a name that is meant to comfort the parents of the child. One name that the researcher came across in the Tangwena area is *Chakupa* which in the other Shona varieties is rendered as *Charakupa*.

Among the Manyika in the study area, this is the only name that was found to be rare. It is also given as *Chakupadenga*. At its fullest the name is given as *Chakupadengahachirambwi*. What it means is that "what the Heavens have given to someone cannot be refused or rejected." The name's theophoric function comes out when it is realised that the purpose of its being given is to comfort the aggrieved that in this case are the parents that are being comforted as well as being encouraged to accept and care for their child that has been given to them by their Creator. This name is also significant in that it does away with the western fiction that the Shona did not care about their disabled. Folk wisdom through proverbs and folktales bears witness to the fact that this is not true.

Another name that has a meaning that is similar to *Chakupa* and that may be given in similar circumstances is *Chaitamwari* (What God has done). At its fullest it is *Chaitamwarihachikanukwi* or *Chaitamwarihachirambwi* (What God has done cannot be looked down at or What God has done cannot be rejected). This name is cautioning that since all people are God's creations, no one has the right to take him to task for what he decides to give to them as a child, whether crippled, blind, albino or any type of deformity that people may be uncomfortable with.

The Christian faith has taken long to be established on the African continent. Despite the claims by theologians that this faith has always been part and parcel of African belief systems since the beginning of the New Testament period or even earlier, indications on the ground are to the contrary, and in any case they do not refer to the area South of the Sahara, may be with the exception of Ethiopia. According to the British Broadcasting Corporation (BBC) the Christian religion first arrived in North Africa (which is Arab dominated), in the first or early second century AD (CE). It is interesting to observe that according to the BBC the Christian communities in North Africa were among the earliest in the world.[16] This is also confirmed by the All About Religion website that states:

> The history of Christianity in Africa probably began during the earthly ministry of Jesus Christ, two thousand years ago. The New Testament of the Bible mentions several events in which Africans were witnesses to the life of Christ and the ministry of the apostles. It is possible that the history of Christianity in Africa began when these Africans shared what they witnessed with other Africans.[17]

As has already been observed, the Africa that is referred to is Arab Africa. It is not Black Africa. The Gospel of Luke even records that Simon of Cyrene was compelled to carry Jesus' cross. But the problem however is to do with the race of Simon. Was he Black or Arab? Christianity spread to as far east as Ethiopia and later suffered a setback as a result of the expansion of Islam. It came to Southern Africa with the Portuguese in the sixteenth century. Gonçalo da Silveira, a Society of Jesus (Jesuit) missionary was arguably the first Christian preacher in southern Africa. He reached the Mutapa's court on Christmas Eve in 1560 and on 15 March 1561, he was killed by the Mutapa's men (Maenzanise 2008: 69). It is important to note that ever since, preachers have

---

[16] http://www.bbc.co.uk/worldservice/africa/features/storyofafrica/index_section8.shtml

[17] http://www.allaboutreligion.org/history-of-christianity-in-africa-faq.htm

been struggling to convert people to Christianity, more than 450 years after. It is in the light of the above observation that the researcher notes that some of the people who convert to Christianity today give their children names that are a message to their unconverted relatives to accept their faith. One of the names that people give to their children is *Gamuchirai* (Receive/ Accept).

The name *Gamuchirai* in reality means convert to Christianity. It is an exhortation to the 'unrepentant' to 'see the light'. In full, the name is *Gamuchiraishe* or *Gamuchiraimwari* (Receive the Lord/ Accept the Lord). Implied in the name is the idea that those who do not repent and accept in Christian terms, Jesus Christ as their Saviour are doomed. From a linguistic perspective, the name *Gamuchiraishe* is also an imperative clause. According to Chalker and Weiner (1994: 197) the term imperative is both a noun and adjective:

(A form or structure) that expresses a command, specifically

a) The base form of the verb when used to express a request, command, order, exhortation, etc.; in the *imperative mood*, ...

b) A complete clause in which the main verb is in the imperative mood. Where a distinction is made between form and function in the analysis of sentence types, *imperative* is a formal category along with DECLARATIVE, INTERROGATIVE, and EXCLAMATIVE. Its discourse is often, but not always that of the DIRECTIVE.

The above words are therefore pertinent in our understanding of some theophoric names as speech acts because as can be observed, some are expressions of commands, orders or directives that for example, people have to accept the Christian God as theirs. What makes the name *Gamuchiraishe* fall into such a category is that it is subtly forcing people to convert to the Christian faith and as is well known about most preachers, they threaten people with eternal death and the unquenchable fires of hell if they do not accept Christianity as their faith.

Vimbainashe (Trust in the Lord) is also another name that has the same function of encouraging other people to turn to the Christian God. The name may possibly have come about as a result of some Christians who after having suffered some calamities may have opted out of the faith, an act that the Christians themselves call backtracking and the others would give children such names as means of telling them not to lose hope in their Lord. This theophoric name is also encouraging non-Christians to convert to the Christian faith. This name may also be interpreted as a living sermon to the non-converted to accept Christianity as the only religion that can bring redemption into their lives.

Christians believe that they have to follow the teaching of Jesus Christ on living exemplary lives. They take this from what Jesus Christ is said to have taught to his disciples during the Sermon on the Mount (Matt 5-7) where Jesus in Matthew 5: 3-4 told his disciples that they were the salt of the earth as well as the light of the world. In this teaching he emphasized that those who did not live a life that reflected that they had received his teaching were as good as people who had not been converted, just like salt that had lost its saltiness that deserved to be thrown away. This allegory which is metaphorical is summarised in the name *Tendekai*. This name is derived from the Shona verb –*tendeka* which means being trustworthy. So when a child is given the theophoric anthroponym *Tendekai,* it can be realised that this is a message that is meant for fellow Christians who are being encouraged to live lives that are blameless, but ones that would bring glory and honour to their God. The namer possibly also hopes that if Christians are exemplary, then more people may convert to their faith. The name is also a reminder even to the members of the namers' family that they should also live upright lives so that the unconverted would learn from them what it means to be a Christian. Such a name is important especially in this day and age where some Christians are accused especially by the Pentecostal denominations of being 'Sunday morning' Christians.

An additional religious name that is linked to *Tendekai* but is targeted at those who are not yet converted is *Tendeukai.* This name is derived from the verb *–tendeuka* which means to turn around and face another direction. In Shona the English word 'convert' has been translated as *'tendeuka'.* So when a child is named *Tendeukai,* this is a call to the not converted to heed the teaching of the preachers to accept Christianity as a redemptive faith. Like *Tendekai,* the name is also an imperative clause that has a subtle threat, that if those who are non-believers in the Christian faith do not convert, then they are doomed. These names clearly show that at times preachers go about their job in a threatening manner. The problem that those who do not believe is that at times these threats are embodied in the names of the children of these preachers, who see in their children reminders of what may happen to the non-believers whom they will always visit or preach to in public places when time allows. The tragedy is that some people may refuse converting to such faiths if they feel that preachers are using their children's names to attempt to convert them in a manner that they consider to be as good as trying to blackmail them.

Conclusion

This chapter has observed that theophoric names are used as reflections of the Christian faith by those Manyika who have accepted it. It has noted that theophoric names in the colonial period were those of saints. Those of the indigenous people were not considered heathen. Conversion as has been brought out in this chapter meant migrating from an African name and the adoption of a Christian one which was either from the bible or a European one. It has as well been noted in this chapter that changes in Christian naming patterns came about with the emergence of nationalism in Zimbabwe. With the advent of independence in 1980, some of the blacks appropriated the Christian faith and to show their acceptance of this faith they ended up giving their children indigenous names. The names that they have given to their children carry their faith, and they reflect aspects such as accepting death as a God-given, and this is summed up in the statement *'Kufa murau waMwari'* (Death is God's law). Some of the names that are given to children carry messages of gratitude as is given in the examples *Tatenda* and *Tinotenda*. There are yet other theophoric names that have a celebratory mood. Names such as *Isheanotida*, *Anotidaishe* and *Tadiwanashe* are in this category. Other names such as *Takudzwanashe* are celebrations as well as boasts. The chapter has as well shown that some names besides boasting are also declaratives. They are the converted's means of publicising to the world that no human being for example, is a victor but God alone. This is fully summed up in the name *Mukundindishe*. Through the very theophoric names, the chapter has as well noted that there are some names that comfort people and advise them to accept their predicament which they perceive as a product of God's action. This is exemplified in names such as *Chaitamwari* and *Chakupa*. The names *Gamuchirai* and Vimbainashe have also been noted to be encouragements as well as means of threatening the non-believers to accept the Christian faith. In addition to all these, the chapter has also noted that some names are living signs of preachers and believers' faith where they are used either as a means of encouraging people who are not yet Christians to embrace the faith, or to those who are already converted to remain steadfast. The next chapter discusses the sentential *Chimurenga* names (*noms de guerre*) that were used by liberation war fighters who operated in the areas under study.

Chapter V

Chimurenga names

Introduction

Pfukwa (2008: 240) decries the fact that there is a dearth in the study of war names in Zimbabwe. He unfortunately does not state whether names of guerrillas have also been studied in countries that waged liberation wars such as Angola and Mozambique as well as Cape Verde and Guinea Bissau. This chapter seeks to add on to the literature that relates to that area in Zimbabwe, and unfortunately it is only limited to sentential names and therefore does not make a claim to be filling that huge void. It is a little but major contribution to an area that still has a lot that has to be unravelled especially as relates to the names that guerrillas who were operating under ZIPRA are concerned. These war names are in Zimbabwe referred to as *Chimurenga* names. The term *Chimurenga* is derived from *Murenga Soro Renzou*. *Murenga* is derived from the verb *–renga* a term which means to cause to act in a harmful way. *Murenga Soro Renzou*, is a name that was derived from the name of a Zimbabwean chief of the Munhumutapa Dynasty, *Murenga Soro Renzou* (Pfukwa and Barnes 2010: 210). According to Mutswairo (researchers' memory of his lectures in the late 1980s) *Murenga Soro Renzou* and *Nyamhangambiri* (One who used and had two swords as well as *Chihweshure* (One who sliced them with swords) were fighters of repute in the pre-colonial Shona period. From this name, it is clear that he was a fighter of repute and so those who embarked in the first *Chimurenga* against white rule (1893-96/7) had the story of this gallant fight at the back of their minds. The fighters of the 1970s liberation war also christened their fight against the Smith regime *Chimurenga*, but they added II to it, indicating that it was a continuation of the war that was left as unfinished business in 1896. According to Pfukwa and Barnes (2010: 210, also citing Lan 1985, Bhebe 1999, Bhebe and Ranger 1995):

Amongst the guerrillas the conflict became known as *Chimurenga*, harkening back to the earlier wars of resistance to British rule (1893–1896). This local name reflected the passion and intensity of feeling towards the conflict described, as it carried a long history.

To the blacks, they were continuing with unfinished business. This understanding that the blacks had about their war is further confirmed by Lohman and MacPherson (1983: 7) who opine with reference to the Zimbabwe war of liberation that "throughout the course of history, the final defeat of one party to a conflict usually sows the seeds of the next conflagration." Even though the two are referring to the 1893 Anglo-Ndebele War, and the 1896-7 War that followed, their words are still relevant to Chimurenga II because it was again as the Nationalists saw it, a carryover from the war that their ancestors had lost.

The Ndebele used the term *Imfazo* to refer to the same war. In this war, the fighters assumed new names for different reasons, but prominent among them was the need to hide their identity because they feared that their relatives and parents back home in Zimbabwe would be victimised by the Rhodesian government if the Rhodesian security forces learnt that they had a child or relative who was a guerrilla.

The guerrillas also assumed new names as an attempt to realign themselves to the new political reality that they were now faced with as they re-entered the country that they had left when they went for military training. Most of these names were assumed at training camps in Mozambique, although those who got trained at the front also got these names. The other people who got these names or gave themselves these *Chimurenga* names were the *mujibhas* and *chimbwidos* (male and female collaborators) who assisted the guerrillas logistically and in reconnaissance activities as well as transport troops that carried weapons from one area to another as the guerrillas penetrated further into the country as their front expanded.

The Second *Chimurenga/Imfazo* was waged against the white colonial and settler government by both the Zimbabwe African National Union (ZANU) through its army the Zimbabwe African National Liberation Army (ZANLA) and the Zimbabwe African People's Union (ZAPU), through the Zimbabwe People's Revolutionary Army (ZIPRA) under the auspices of the Patriotic Front (PF). This study however, focuses only on guerrillas from ZANU's armed wing ZANLA because these are the ones who operated in the areas that are under study, and specifically only on sentential names.

Naming and/in the war of liberation

Between 1964 (1966 according to some sources such as Pfukwa [2010, 2008, 2007), himself an ex-ZANLA combatant) and 1979 (Raeburn 1981, Lohman and MacPherson 1983), Zimbabwe, (then Rhodesia) experienced a bitter military struggle that pitted black versus white. This armed struggle started off as a low intensity war in 1964 with the activities of the Crocodile Gang in Chimanimani (then Melsetter). This guerrilla outfit was the first one to have killed a white person since the 1896-7 War in which both the Ndebele and Shona had been defeated. There is no history about how the name Crocodile Gang came about, but it is a name that carried with it the idea of completely annihilating the enemy. It may also be a result of the influence of Shona wisdom that is captured in the proverb *Ngwena haidyi chebamba, chayo chinoza neronga* (A crocodile does not grab that which it eats, but that which comes by the river). This means that a crocodile lies in wait for its meal. It does not go out and hunt as do the other animals such as lions and leopards. This behaviour is typical of guerrilla units. They set up ambushes at appropriate places and lie in wait for the target to appear. They then hit and run away, and again wait for a more opportune time to strike.

The naming of military units is not something new. The Rhodesian Army had units that had names such as Buffalo, a reference to the army unit that was based in Mutare (then Umtali). ZANU also developed a system where each year was named, with certain objectives and it was these objectives that had to be politically and militarily met in a particular year. For example, 1978 was called the Year of the People (*Gore reVanhu*) and 1979 was the Year of the Storm (*Gore reGukurahundi*). In pre-colonial wars people also got names that came about as a result of their prowess in battle. Among the Ndebele, one such fighter was Mkhithika whose family name is Thebe but because he managed to kill so many people in battle he got the name *Mkhithika*. Legend has it that he was fearless and he would venture into the midst of the enemy forces and stab them and they would fall down like leaves falling from a tree (*ukukhithika*) (Interview with Simangenkosi Thebe 15 February 2013). Pfukwa (2007: 59) confirms the use of war names as recent as during the Second World War when he cites the case of the Jedburghs that supported the resistance movements in France and Belgium and also in South East Asia where they took undercover names, especially when they operated in their own countries. War names were also used in the Vietnam War (Pfukwa 2007: 59).

The war of liberation was initially a disaster because both ZANU and ZAPU spent more time fighting one another than engaging the enemy that the guerrillas they sent to the front were not adequately prepared and most were soon caught by the Rhodesian security forces and tried and hanged since the Smith regime considered them criminals. Their activities were uncoordinated and amateurish (Lohman and MacPherson 1983: 17). There was however a dramatic change when ZANU opened a new front in north eastern Zimbabwe in 1972 when there was an attack on Christmas Eve Altena Farm (Martin and Johnson 1981).

It is important to note that in the early stages of the war ZANU's military wing ZANLA had relied on press-ganging, a strategy that ZAPU was later to resort to as well, in an effort to swell her ranks of recruits and fighters (Raeburn 1981; Makari 1985, 1992, 2003). By the mid1970s ZANLA had so many willing recruits that joined her ranks as a result of her political education that was carried out at the front through all night teachings (*pungwes*). Those who enlarged the ranks of ZANLA on departing from their homes and on entering refugee and training camps, or on undergoing military training at the front, as ZANLA later resorted to in the last stages of the war, assumed new names that were in line with

115

their new vocation and call. Besides acting as a cover against possible reprisals that would befall their relatives and families at the hands of the Rhodesian security forces (Tungamirai 1995: 45), the *Chimurenga* names as well functioned in some instances as a call to arms for the Zimbabwean people, or as a call to the generality of the masses to give all kinds of support to the guerrillas, and through these guerrillas to the armed struggle that was meant to liberate the country. These guerrilla names were in addition a reflection of the combatants' new political awareness as well as their new role in the struggle to liberate the country from the shackles of racism (Tungamirai 1995: 45). They were both expressive and declarative statements as well as commissives. The guerrilla names therefore had different shades of meaning, but the meanings carried in each of the names were meant to be motivators to both the guerrillas and the masses to commit themselves to the Second *Chimurenga/Imfazo*, because this was perceived as the only means available to ending white settler hegemony.

It is essential to point out here that when a person assumed a new name as a guerrilla, that name was an act of renaming as well as reinsertion in history, but this time around as one of the movers of history and not its subject. By getting a new name one was reclaiming his or her political space. Pfukwa (2007: 49) notes that it is necessary that guerrilla names be understood in the context of the circumstances that led to the coming of the Second *Chimurenga*, arguing that guerrilla names are associative because they are loaded with political, social and cultural emotions.

Guerrilla Sentential Names

When people joined the war of liberation, they assumed new identities that were characterized by changes in names. These names that they bore were of great significance to both the bearers and the masses among whom these guerrillas operated. Pfukwa (2012) has categorised these names into thirteen groups that range from the semantically transparent to miscellaneous ones. As he discusses the names he also just gives the meaning of the name. It is only in very few cases that he thoroughly discusses a name. This chapter, unlike what Pfukwa does, is narrower in its approach in that it focuses on names that are complete statements only. These may be made up of one word or more, and they may be verbal or a combination of the verbal and the substantival. In this chapter the researcher only discusses fourteen war names. These are not the only ones, but with limited time and space he believes that these are representative is enough in that they give some insight into the type of messages that the guerrillas relayed to their fellow comrades-in-arms, the masses and the white Rhodesian community as well as their black collaborators.

The names of the guerrillas that are discussed in this chapter are of those combatants who operated in Nyanga district (also known among ZANLA combatants as Chitepo Sector), in Nyamaropa, Katerere, at Bende, as well as Tangwena and Nyatate areas. They also operated in Mutasa district. These guerrillas may have stayed for a long period or may have been in transit into the interior of the country into areas such as Makoni and Macheke. So many guerrillas passed through this area, but these among the other are the ones that had names that were in their own way outstanding to the researcher. This is because all these guerrilla names are statements in miniature.

Wars are by nature destructive. They mean loss of life to either combatant. Such gruesome reality requires some form of psychological shock absorbers. Some of the shock absorbers that the guerrillas used include the names that they were given or those that they gave themselves in an effort to keep at bay chances of death and injury as well as the possibility of capture and torture by enemy forces whose prospects were always a looming likelihood. It is in such situations that names like *Bataihana* (Do not panic/ Do not divulge secrets) were given and came into play. This *nom de guerre*, *Bataihana* which is an imperative speech act because it gives orders has four possible meanings. The first two possible meanings relate to the guerrillas. In a battle situation or in a state of affairs where the guerrillas were being tracked by Rhodesian security forces and were in hiding, there was always need for the guerrillas not to panic. They had to remain calm and in hiding. If one panicked, there was the potential danger he would break cover and expose himself and probably others to possible death, capture and torture as well as face trial in a country whose judiciary system did not treat captured guerrillas as political and military people but as common criminals.

The name may also have been a call to the guerrillas to remain level and cool headed in the heat of battle. It was a reminder that they had to keep collected, especially when they were under enemy fire. Given the fact that guerrilla armies were made up of people of different age groups, as well as veterans and amateurs, this name had the function of being a confidence builder, especially to those who had recently been deployed to the front.

The third possible meaning of the name *Bataihana* is that it functioned as a message that was directed at the majority of the masses. Guerrillas in most cases came at dusk or at night. They did not want their presence to be known to most people, especially children and other suspicious ones. They did also not want people who were visitors to a particular area to know about them or their whereabouts. In the circumstances, it can be observed that the name is an imperative statement in addition to it being a directive. The people were being compelled and directed to keep information about the guerrillas in their area a closely guarded secret. The significance of secrecy to most guerrilla armies and depending on their location is underscored by Ernesto Che Guevara who states:

> This popular work should at first be aimed at securing secrecy; that is, each peasant, each member of the society in which action is taking place, will be asked not to mention what he sees and hears; ... (1961: 16).

These words succinctly put across what was prevailing in the operational areas in the days of the liberation struggle. It is however, important to point out that it was only towards the end of the war and in areas that the guerrillas considered liberated that their presence was no longer kept a secret.

It did happen at times that some guerrillas got caught in battle when they were involved in engagements with the Rhodesian security forces. Because it is known that some captured guerrillas did break under torture, the name *Bataihana* is also an appeal to fellow guerrillas as well as collaborators (*mujibhas*) to suffer and die in silence even if the torture is unbearable, in the unlikely event that they got caught by the Rhodesian forces. They were not to reveal the locations of their base camps, supporters as well as sites of their arms caches.

Rangarirai Magorira (Remember/ Consider the guerrillas) is one of the guerrillas who operated for a very long time in the Nyamaropa-Katerere area in Nyanga district. He was affectionately known as Comrade *Ranga*. The researcher gathered that he had grown up in the Katerere area and his civilian name was *Augustine Rangarirai Mabvira* (Maxwell 1995; 1993: 367). He only dropped his family name Mabvira and replaced it with *Magorira* (Guerrillas). By assuming this name *Rangarirai* was confirming and reasserting the fact that his name was not just a text that was carrying the war story, but in it was embedded the history of resistance to a political system that disadvantaged the majority of the Zimbabwean population (Pfukwa and Barnes 2010: 209). He already bore the name *Rangarirai* that he had got from his parents, a sign that for him and his parents, the act of onomastic erasure had already been embarked on since they had not given him a western name as had become the trend under colonial rule. When looked at in its fullest, as *Rangarirai Magorira* the name becomes a complete statement, and as used in the war situation the name may have been an appeal to the masses to really rally behind the guerrillas by giving them logistical and reconnaissance as well as intelligence support. The name may also mean that the masses had to take the guerrillas as their sons and daughters, as well as brothers and sisters, so in the event that people decided to withdraw their assistance to the liberation war fighters they had to think twice.

The name *Rangarirai Magorira* was also an appeal to fellow combatants to always remember why they were in the bush and the reason the war of liberation had to be fought. They as well had to remember the injustices that the white settler regime had perpetrated on the blacks, and how some of the laws that they had enacted had disadvantaged the majority blacks in the land of their birth. Even the masses also had to remember why the war had to be fought although some of them may have been persuaded through intimidation tactics to support the guerrillas and their war effort. The importance of the need for the guerrillas to be 'remembered' and be considered with favour is highlighted in the Sri Lankan blog site that states:

> A friendly population is of immense importance to guerrilla fighters, providing shelter, supplies, financing, intelligence and recruits. The 'base of the people' is thus the key lifeline of the guerrilla movement.

It is clear from these words that the name *Rangarirai Magorira* was a silent and enduring prayer to the masses to continue supporting the guerrillas through the continued provision of basic necessities that would make the guerrillas' stay in the bush tolerable.

In Shona tradition there are taboos that give the dos and don'ts that relate to hunters and sexual relations. People were for example, not allowed to eat vegetables such as pumpkin leaves as well as to indulge in sexual relations at the war front. The reasons that relate to pumpkin leaves and sexual intimacy are linked to dietary concerns and security, that the guerrillas called 'vigilance'. In his study (Mapara 2010: 19-30) noted that pumpkin leaves are not good enough because they tend to have sand and small stones attached to them especially at the height of the summer season. There was also the danger therefore that one was not likely to enjoy his or her meal and

121

was not likely to be satiated. This was not good in a war situation where a contact had chances of occurring at any time and there was as well the possibility that when such an occurrence did take place there was also the likelihood that one could go for days without food. It is clear therefore that this name may have also been given with the idea of minimising the chances of the guerrillas getting away famished. It was in the light of such possibilities that the masses had also to consider the issue of relish when dealing with the guerrillas, hence the name *Rangarirai Magorira*.

As regards sexual liaisons at the war front, the name was an appeal to both the guerrillas as well as their collaborators to refrain from such an energy sapping act. In a war situation it also has to be noted that security of the self and the entire group is of paramount importance. The sexual act itself is very absorbing. If one was to engage in it while on guard duty, in the event of the enemy encroaching close to the camp, the chances of escaping by the guerrillas were reduced, with the guerrillas being put on the defensive, when ideally guerrilla armies should be on the offensive.

Most of the guerrillas were very religious, subscribing to either African Traditional Religion (ATR) or Christianity. During the war of liberation in Zimbabwe this reality was reflected even in some of the names that the guerrillas bore. One guerrilla whose name was a religious message was *Tendai Vadzimu* (Give thanks to the ancestral spirits/ Be grateful to the ancestral spirits). For the period when the liberation war was on, there was a belief among some guerrillas that the war they were fighting had the backing of the ancestral spirits. In the Shona religion, ancestors are believed to operate at three levels that are namely: the family, the ethnic (tribal) as well as national levels. They are at all levels perceived as the guardians of the land. In short, the land belongs to them and the chiefs preside over it on their behalf. To the guerrillas, Zimbabwe was therefore a land of the ancestral spirits. When the white colonialists curved out farms for themselves, they did this not from the land of the Shona and Ndebele whom they had defeated, but from the land's ancestral spirits. The blacks therefore believed that the day of reckoning for the whites would one day come. The name *Tendai Vadzimu* was as a result a reminder to the masses as well as fellow guerrillas to always remember that they had to thank the ancestors whose bones had risen in the form of the guerrillas to reclaim their land from the whites and the freedom of their people.

The name also played a significant role within the guerrilla ranks such that during the war of liberation the medium of Nehanda was relocated to Mozambique (Makari 1985; Tungamirai 1995). This is important because it boosted the morale of the guerrillas. Some of the guerrillas believed that they had to defer to the ancestral spirits because they had faith that it was them who looked after them in the bush and ensured their success against white Rhodesian forces. Chung (2006: 197) reiterates the importance of the belief that the guerrillas had in ancestral spirits in Zimbabwe's liberation war when she comments:

One of the most striking characteristics of the Zimbabwean liberation struggle was the power of traditional religious leaders, the *vana sekuru*. They held a special position in the psyche of the freedom fighters; particularly the peasant soldiers who constituted about half the freedom fighters.

Although Chung is of the opinion that the belief is something that affected the mostly peasant soldiers of ZANLA, she errs to conclude that the belief in the role of ancestral spirits in the life of guerrillas only affected the poorly educated. The reality about the Shona and even other Bantus in Zimbabwe like the Kalanga and Ndebele is that even though most profess to be believers and followers of the Christian faith, there are times in their lives when they revert to African Traditional Religion, especially when they would have faced problems. So when one gave himself a name such as *Tendai Vadzimu*, or was given that name by colleagues, he was saying or accepting that the ancestors' role in the conduct and progress of the war of liberation against the enemy forces was to be acknowledged.

It is important to note that during the 1970s when the war of liberation escalated, most rural areas had been infiltrated by the Christian religion. However, among the chiefs, there were many who though tolerant to Christian practices, were followers and believers as well as practitioners of African Traditional Religion (ATR). The chiefs followed this religion for political reasons because they deferred to ancestral spirits especially when it came to the issue of ascending to the office of chief. The name *Tendai Vadzimu* then becomes a call to both the guerrillas and the masses in ensuring that the belief in the role the ancestral spirits were playing in the struggle for Zimbabwe would not die. It is because of the belief in the ancestral spirits' resilience that the guerrillas now found themselves fighting against the white Rhodesian settler forces.

The name *Tichatonga* (We shall rule [the country]) is an expression of hope that the guerrillas had that blacks would one day run the affairs of the country. Its hope for the future rule by blacks is summed up in the tense indicator *–cha–* that is in the name *Tichatonga* which can be morphologically presented as:

$$\emptyset\text{- } + \text{-ti- } + \text{-cha- } + \text{-tong- } + \text{- a}$$

np   sc   ts   VR   tv

The above shows that the name *Tichatonga* which belongs to class 1a and like all the other personal names that are complex it is made up of several constituents which in this case are the noun prefix (np), the subject concord (sc), the tense sign or tense indicator (ts) and the verb radicle or root (VR) as well as the terminal vowel (tv). The name is an elliptical statement of a sentence that may possibly have read or sounded *Tichatonga isu vatema* or *Isu vatema tichatonga* (Us, the blacks are going to rule). From the speech act theory it functions as a declarative. As a grammatical entity it falls within the category where it is written without a subject which in this case is first person plural. This as a rule in Bantu languages is not normally included unless someone is speaking with emphasis. The name *Tichatonga* therefore stands alone as a declarative statement where the blacks as represented by this guerrilla are openly and defiantly telling the whites in Rhodesia and the world at large that the blacks will ultimately assume the reins of power in Zimbabwe. This name therefore fulfils Pfukwa and Barnes' (2010: 211) observation that *Chimurenga* names are a product of a wider social discourse that is often influenced by bitterness and mutual dislike. This is exactly the case that was prevailing in colonial Rhodesia. The socio-political and economic environment was poisoned by so much hate and loathing of one another between the blacks and whites. The calamity is that earlier on Ian Smith had once declared:

I don't believe in Black Majority rule ever – not in a thousand years. I repeat that what I believe in is Black and

White working together. I believe that if one day we have white rule and the next black rule then we will have failed and that will be a disaster for Rhodesia.[18]

These words, especially the part 'not in a thousand years' have been interpreted to mean that the whites were not prepared to relinquish power. This seems to be confirmed by Smith himself in his biography *The Great Betrayal* (2007). It is a result of this seeming intransigence that black nationalists decided to embark on an armed struggle through guerrilla activities and this is where names like *Tichatonga* came out. It is a name that was intended to motivate its bearer and his comrades as well as the masses to focus on the struggle against white rule because as far as the guerrillas were concerned victory was certain, what was not clear was when it would be achieved.

The Rhodesian propaganda machinery had worked so much on most blacks especially those in the rural areas in the psychological arena. This led most blacks to believe that the whites were invincible. In some cases the white Rhodesian forces displayed the captured guerrillas as well as bodies of those they would have killed in battle. At other times they showed films and pictures of slain guerrillas. Most of the pictures and even the display of corpses were done to young children and youths, especially in schools in an effort to discourage them from supporting and joining the guerrilla armies. It is with this background in mind that names such as *Tichatonga* came up. Through this name, the bearer is informing the masses who were the major target of the Rhodesian Psychological War (Psyops) that while there were set-backs in the fight against the settler forces, victory was

---

[18] http://en.wikiquote.org/wiki/Ian_Smith

inevitable and it was within sight. It was therefore a call to the majority of the masses to be brave even when there were situations when it appeared as if the guerrillas were losing ground. Some blacks also ended up believing what the Rhodesian government peddled as the truth because from 1964, the Rhodesian Broadcasting Corporation, a statutory body, came under tighter control from the government. The situation was also worsened by the fact by the mid-1970s, the Rhodesian authorities also commissioned frequency modulation (FM) transmitters as well as transistor radios that received on transmission through FM. This was done in an effort to counter the British Broadcasting Corporation (BBC) as well as extra-territorial radio stations that were beaming on Rhodesia from Dar es Salaam, Lusaka, Maputo and Moscow that hosted the liberation movements ZANU and ZAPU.

It is essential to note that the war of liberation called for psychological warfare from both sides. While the Rhodesians were using radio and dropping by plane leaflets on the rural population that was the bulwark of the guerrillas, the guerrillas also responded by broadcasting from foreign lands as well as by attacking farms and other strategic installations. For the white communities, the major casualties of the war were the farmers who were based in areas that were in most cases surrounded by rural areas or were very close to the rural areas. Some areas were near forestry plantations. Most of the farms that became targets of the guerrillas were largely in border areas or in provinces that shared a common boundary with Mozambique that was the ZANU's rear base. Grundy and Miller (1979)[19] note this when they record that between 1973 and 1979 about 275 farmers and/or with their children died in the war. They go on to state that this number does

[19] www.rhodesia.nl/farmeratwar.html

127

not include the names of the sons of the farmers that were killed on active duty with the Rhodesian security forces. It is possibly with this knowledge, of the death toll that was rising among the white farmers in mind that gave some guerrillas space to give themselves names such as *Mabhunu Muchapera* (Boers, you shall perish). What this name means is that the Boers or farmers (a term used to refer to all whites although etymologically it means whites of Afrikaner origin) who were the bulk of the Rhodesian agriculturalists were going to be continuously decimated by the guerrilla armies.

It is also equally true that Rhodesian farmers suffered heavy casualties at the hands of the guerrillas. These went as far back as 1964 when the Crocodile Gang unleashed its wrath on the farmers of Melsetter (now Chimanimani) by killing Pieter Oberholzer (Ranger 1997: 273). Most of the farmers in the eastern districts of Manicaland moved away, a fact that is again confirmed by Grundy and Miller (1979)[20]. The two writers however note that most of the farmers in the north east of the country, around Mount Darwin stayed put on their properties.

During the war for Zimbabwe's independence one of the issues that were always raised by most guerrillas was that after the attainment of majority rule, which they argued was not negotiable whites were going to be chased out of the country. Those who remained behind were going to become slaves of the blacks. It was also stated that those who had been cruel to the blacks such as farmers were going to face the firing squad, or the masses were going to be given a chance and the joy of killing them painfully by removing their limbs one-by-one. Such guerrilla propaganda may also have led some to give themselves names such as *Mabhunu Muchapera*.

---

[20] www.rhodesia.nl/farmeratwar.html

128

Not everyone who joined the war of liberation did so because of the zeal to liberate the country from oppression and racism. Some joined the ranks of the guerrillas because they wanted to inflict revenge on the whites whom they felt had done them an injustice by for example, either killing their father or even humiliating them (as Weeds Chakarakata [That which burns the throat] alias Gonese) did after independence because his father had been branded during the war by a farmer in Masvingo's Gutu district (interview with the late Cosmas Gonese 16 September 2010) and fictionalised by Makari in the novel *Zvaida Kushinga* (1985, 1992). It is people like these who joined the guerrilla ranks who may also have given themselves names such as *Mabhunu Muchapera* in an effort to inspire themselves as well as to threaten the whites that they were going to be massacred by the guerrillas. The masses unfortunately never had chances to ask questions on how these names came about. All they did was to think into what each name a guerrilla carried in that particular context. Such names are in tandem with Pfukwa and Barnes (2010: 211) who observe that war names were a medium through which feelings were expressed as shown by some of the ethnic slurs that reflect the bitterness of the conflict. *Mabhunu Muchapera* definitely one such name because it carries in it some racial slur.

Teurai Ropa (now Joice Mujuru, co-Vice President in the Government of Zimbabwe) never set foot in Nyanga as a combatant. Her name is however being discussed in this chapter because it is one of the names that were always coming up in all night political teachings that ZANLA guerrillas carried out in most of the rural areas that were under the control of ZANLA forces. Most of these were what ZANU and ZANLA called either liberated zones or semi-liberated zones, terms that were used to mean that the Rhodesian security forces feared to venture into them or if they did, they quickly withdrew. *Teurai Ropa* was at the height of the liberation struggle Secretary for Women's Affairs as well as a member of the Central Committee of ZANU. *Teurai Ropa* is the *nom de guerre* of one Joice Runaida Mugari who later became Mujuru after getting married to Solomon Mujuru. According to Africa Confidential, she earned the name *Teurai Ropa* (Spill blood) after having downed a helicopter in 1974.[21] It is therefore clear that she did not give herself the name, but it is one that was given her by those who appreciated her feat.

The name *Teurai Ropa* is a justification of the war of liberation. In it are carried undertones of a statement that seems to have been at that time declaring that the war of liberation was a just war that required that blood be shed so as to attain majority rule. In this context the name was making it clear that the killing of Rhodesian security forces, as well as their spouses, children and supporters was necessary for the attainment of majority rule and the removal of oppression. According to the Internet Encyclopedia of Philosophy[22] just war is based on the following principles: having a just cause, being a last resort, being declared by a proper authority, possessing right intention, having a reasonable chance of success, and the end being proportional to the means used. While some of the principles are highly contestable, Zimbabwe's war of liberation may be considered to have been justifiable at least on three of the principles. These three are having a just cause, being a last resort and possessing the right intention.

---

[21] www.africa-confidential.com/whos-who-profile/id/3046
[22] www.iep.utm.edu/justwar/

Blacks were fighting against racism and oppression as well as for political inclusion. So the war was just and blood as *Teurai Ropa* the name suggests, had to be spilt so as to attain this objective. The blacks had also tried to get involved politically and to have a majority representation in government since they were demographically more than the whites in the country but this was in vain. If anything, in response to the demands of the blacks, the white rulers of Rhodesia responded by incarcerating and banishing the nationalist leaders to detention centres in the least hospitable parts of the country. At the end the blacks decided to embark on an armed struggle as the only option available to them. It is again clear according to one of the principles of a just war, that the armed struggle became a means of last resort and it was therefore justifiable that blood be spilt for the attainment of majority rule. The blood that the blacks saw as necessary to spill was that of the whites, hence the name *Teurai Ropa*. The war of liberation was also justifiable because it was fought with the right intention. Even though it is a revolution that went off track after independence, the idea of entrenching majority rule was not bad. It also therefore means that it was again necessary that blood be spilt for these right intentions to be fulfilled.

The name *Teurai Ropa* may also have been an open call to blacks to take up arms and topple the white minority regime because of its unyieldingness and in some cases in point high handedness and cruelty. It is important to note that from a psychological perspective, names have a powerful effect on the behaviour of the name bearer (Hargreaves, Colman and Slunkin 1983: 394). They further state that among the Ashanti children are named according to the day of the week on which they are born, and there is a widespread consensus among the Ashanti that these names are strongly associated with personality. Thus Monday boys are supposed to be quiet and well behaved, whereas Wednesday boys are seen as quick-tempered and belligerent (1983: 394). From their observation it is clear that at times names inform behaviour. In the light of this it may also be argued that the name *Teurai Ropa* could likewise have played a significant part in the named's commitment to the liberation struggle. Given the fact that she is said to have downed a helicopter, there was then need to keep her psyched up to be prepared to face the Rhodesian forces and their airpower in the event that she got deployed to the front or even when their training camps came under attack from Rhodesian forces. The name *Teurai Ropa*, even though it was given to her, entrenches and confirms what Pfukwa and Barnes (2010: 211) state when they observe that naming is an act that reflects identity. They go on to also assert that in guerrilla war new identities come about as a result of new ideologies as well as a new awareness or reawakening. It is in the light of this new awareness that one takes up a new name or accepts a new name as a way of doing away with the old self, as well as to project a new self with new knowledge in addition to embracing that new knowledge. That was probably the case with the name *Teurai Ropa*. The bearer had new knowledge about what she could achieve. The name may therefore have motivated her and encouraged her.

While the name *Teurai Ropa* (Spill blood) is about spilling the blood of Rhodesian settlers, there are some names that entrenched the idea of self-sacrifice, and paying the supreme price for the liberation of the country. One such name is *Tafirenyika* (shortened as *Tafi*). The name can be translated as 'We have died for the country/land'. What the name really means is that it is a memorial statement for those who had fallen and were to fall in the struggle to liberate the country. The name therefore shows one's full commitment to the effort to liberate the country. As a speech act, it is a commissive. In short, the name *Tafirenyika* like all the others that were borne by the participants in the war of liberation have functions similar to other names and trademarks in that they:

denote: they provide a shorthand for an entity that can be used by others as a reference. Second, both personal names and trademarks *connote*: they communicate, either directly or by suggestion, certain characteristics about a person or good, whether actual or aspirational. Third, both personal names and trademarks *associate*: they communicate relationships between or among entities through a shared name (Heymann 2011: 392).

Although as already noted, the above quotation refers to both personal names and trademarks. What they state is equally essential when applied to guerrilla names that were used in Zimbabwe's war of liberation. A closer look at the above quotation underscores the fact that the bearer of the *nom de guerre* was prepared to pay the supreme price for the freedom of the majority of the people of his country. The same name communicates the position that the guerrilla had taken: as an individual he was telling his fellow comrades that he personally had taken the decision to die for the country if there was need. Through that same act, he also became a reference point for fellow guerrillas to emulate.

The name *Tafirenyika* is not only directed at the guerrillas. It was as well meant for the encouragement of the masses that had to be brave in the face of adversity that would normally come in the form of arrests, detentions and torture at the hands of the Rhodesian security forces. The name, in a war situation was suggesting that it was better to die alone without betraying fellow comrades and the cause of the war than to die a disgraceful death after having betrayed the liberation war. If one was to do that, such an action would not benefit his or her family, relatives and friends.

It has been indicated in the first chapter and in some of the others that follow that the grammatical structure and semantic function of some or most of the names as speech acts as well discourse analysis forms is clear. Such aspects are found even in some of the *Chimurenga* names. One example of such a name is *Baya Bongozozo*. This *nom de guerre* has both the first name and second name (surname). The first name *Baya* means 'Shoot' and *Bongozozo* means 'Chaos'. What this name therefore possibly means is that the guerrillas had to fight the Rhodesian forces in a manner that would cause chaos in their rank and file, such that they would not know what hit them. They were not only encouraged but also expected to cause chaos and confusion not only in the land but also in the minds of the Rhodesian forces in all their different units, be they farmers on national duty or the professional soldiers.

The name *Baya Bongozozo* was also a subtle order to the masses. During the war of liberation, some of the words that ZANLA forces chanted were as follows:

ZANLA combatant: Muhondo!
Masses: Iwe neni tine basa!

ZANLA combatant: Chimurenga!
Masses: Chekusunungura Zimbabwe!

(ZANLA combatant: In times of war!
Masses: You and I have tasks/duties!
ZANLA combatant: Chimurenga!
Masses: [To be waged] To liberate Zimbabwe!)

The above words show that both the ZANLA forces and the masses had to work together in their effort to liberate Zimbabwe. In such a scenario when one bore a name like *Baya Bongozozo* it is clear that the name like the others that have been discussed above acknowledged that both the guerrillas and the masses were equal partners in the fight against the Rhodesians. The *nom de guerre* was also meant to be a means of encouraging the masses to participate and give the war effort an impetus through acts of sabotage such as filling up dip tanks with rocks, digging up roads so that they became impassable and rustling cattle from white farms. The masses could also poison livestock that was on farms as well torch shops of the whites that were on farms as well as in the rural areas. All the acts of sabotage were meant to demoralise the white farming community and push them out of farming activities so that they would relocate to the urban areas, or even get out of the country. The guerrillas desired the latter, and even Ian Smith (2007) confirms that by the mid to late 1970s, the number of whites who were leaving Rhodesia had risen to alarming proportions. If the interpretation given for this name in the above paragraph carries weight, this name obviously throws away the claim that veterans of Zimbabwe's war of liberation make; that they are the ones who fought for the liberation of the country on their own. They are now being motivated by greed. It is clear that the need to get mass support was motivated by the teachings of Mao who is echoed in Che Guevara who noted that guerrilla warfare is a war of the masses with the guerrillas only playing the role of the vanguard of the people.

Another name that was addressed to both the bearer and fellow combatants is *Kasikai Patiri Pakashata* (Be fast, we are not in a safe place). This name carried with it a sense of urgency. The bearer was reminding his colleagues that they had to act with a sense of swiftness because they were in hostile territory. This need for exigency emanated from may be the earlier days of the guerrilla war when the guerrillas had to keep under cover for long periods without exposing themselves. The name also became a living reminder of what was expected of the masses and fellow guerrillas when they were under attack or when they suspected that they were under surveillance from the Rhodesian forces. They had to move tactfully but fast. The significance of this is immortalised in the teachings of Che Guevara who states:

At the outset, the essential task of the guerrilla fighter is to keep himself from being destroyed. Little by little it will be easier for members of the guerrilla band or bands to adapt themselves to their form of life and make flight and escape from the forces that are on the offensive an easy task, because it is performed daily (1961: 15).

These words confirm that speed was of essence to the guerrillas. If they were not cautious they risked not only capture but also annihilation at the hands of the enemy forces. Even though these words were essential largely for the fighters who were at the front, speed was also an important aspect of the war even in the supply of food because at times guerrillas wanted only food in a particular area and then they would move on to a less hostile area, especially if they were in a situation where the Rhodesian forces were in hot pursuit.

Heymann (2011: 387) is of the opinion that history suggests that naming as a practice developed more as a reference system for others, and not necessarily to reflect personal or spiritual identity fulfilment. Whether as a reference system or for identity and spiritual purposes, what is important about names is that they have a dual function – to identify as well as be a reference point for human beings who are despite their different faiths are largely spiritual beings. One *nom de guerre* that in some way fulfils these attributes (not that others do not) is *Charles Tanganeropa*. This name shows that guerrillas also used western or English names, besides names from other parts of the world. *Charles Tanganeropa* operated in the Nyamaropa-Nyadowa as well as Katerere areas of Nyanga district before he moved on either to Nyatate (also in Nyanga) or Chiendambuya and environs (in Makoni district). His first name is western and it means 'man' or 'manly'. It is difficult to ascertain whether he knew what the first name means. His second name, *Tanganeropa* (You start off by losing or shedding blood) may nevertheless be a pointer to the bearer having been to school where he had studied Shona literature. The name *Tanganeropa* (initially *Tanga*) is that of the major protagonist in the novel *Pfumo Reropa* (Chakaipa 1961). In the novel *Tanga* succeeds on a very difficult and potentially fatal mission. He is pricked and faces a very venomous snake in a thicket where it was hardly possible for a person to manoeuvre. He nonetheless succeeds to get the sapling that was to be used as the handle for his spear (*rwiriko*) but after losing a lot of blood through injury caused by the thorns as he crawled through the thicket. When Haripotse saw him coming out of the grove with his body covered in blood, that is when he rechristened him *Tanganeropa* and he insisted that that was the name was going to use hence.

It is the meaning that is carried in the name *Tanganeropa* that *Charles Tanganeropa* wanted to be associated with. What the name perhaps means was that like the character *Tanganeropa* who had been dispossessed by Ndyire (The greedy and grabbing one), blacks had been dispossessed by the white settlers, who also did this because of their greed and grabbing culture. Like Chakaipa's *Tanganeropa* who rallied the people behind him in the fight against Ndyire II for the hand of Munjai's hand in marriage, this modern *Tanganeropa* was also rallying the majority of the Zimbabwean masses behind him and his fellow comrades in the fight against white Rhodesians who had not only taken away the land of the blacks, but were still continuing doing so (Symbolically Zimbabwe is also Munjai, the woman that Tanganeropa loved very much).

The name *Charles Tanganeropa* may also have meant that as men (most guerrilla units were made up of young men) they had to be manly, that is brave in the face of the Rhodesian military might. Since the blacks had initially in the first *Chimurenga* been bloodied by the occupying forces of the British South Africa Company (BSAC), they were like the *Tanganeropa* in Chakaipa's novel who was initially bloodied by the thicket, but after that incident he is the one who was always the first to draw blood from his adversaries and in the process at all times came out the winner. That is how he became a victor. It was possible that through this character, the namesake, *Charles Tanganeropa* and his comrades-in-arms were equating themselves to the literary dramatis persona and they were stating that they were going to be the ones to always draw the blood of the Rhodesian forces. The guerrillas would draw blood first through acts such as ambushes, the laying and detonating of landmines, and attacking and destroying enemy outposts as well as farms and other strategic installations. Although Che Guevara is discussing the importance of saving arms, his words seem to confirm the meaning in the destruction of the enemy that is embedded in the *nom de guerre Tanganeropa*. Guevara sates:

> The technique of lying in ambush along roads in order to explode mines and annihilate survivors is one of the most remunerative in point of ammunition and arms. The surprised enemy does not use his ammunition and has no time to flee; so with a small expenditure of ammunition large results are achieved (1961: 24).

From the above words, it is clear that the name *Charles Tanganeropa* is indicative of people who followed the Maoist teaching on guerrilla warfare as expounded and modified by Che Guevara.

Linked to the name *Charles Tanganeropa* is *Tambaoga*. Like *Tanganeropa*, this name is also taken from a Shona novel, *Tambaoga Mwana'ngu* (Kuimba 1965). In this novel, *Tambaoga* who is also the protagonist is the son of Chief Mupakaviri who is murdered by his young brother Zinwamhanga. Zinwamhanga's intention is to usurp the throne. He attempts to cover his implication in the murder of his brother by putting the blame for the death on the Chief's first born son *Tambaoga* (Play it alone/ Solve the case on your own my son). However, the Chief spiritually communicates with his son

Tambaoga and Zinwamhanga is exposed, disgraced and killed. Like in the novel, the guerrillas were like *Tambaoga* in the sense that they had to take it upon themselves to liberate the country. The name was also significant to those in the rear bases who had to find means of sustaining recruits as well as children and others in the camps. They did not necessarily have to wait for donations from countries such as those in the Scandinavian region of Western Europe that gave a lot of support especially medicinal and clothing.

The name may also have played a motivating role to the masses in the sense that they had to realise that no one else was going to come to their rescue except themselves working with the guerrillas. They were their own liberators. Examples of the masses doing the act alone include among others the provision of food, bedding and clothing for the guerrillas. The collaborators also acted as the ears and eyes of the guerrillas as they did reconnaissance activities for the guerrillas. Some women collaborators carried parcel bombs that they placed in busy whites' only shopping centres.

The guerrillas and the masses also learnt that they did not have to bank on the outside world to help them fight or resolve issues in their country. They had tried this when they had appealed to different British governments between 1961 and 1976 but this had been to no avail. Conferences had also been held but these had yielded no positive results. They had therefore come to the realisation that no one other than themselves was going to fight their war. It is important to note that when the masses and the guerrillas came to the realisation that they were their own liberators, they were confirming what Che Guevara is said to have at one time stated in 1958 when he, in Mexico made the statement, "I am not a liberator. Liberators do not exist. The people liberate themselves." These words are very telling. They clearly inform us that there is no one in life who will fight another person's battles and wars but his own (en.wikiquote.org/wiki/Ernesto_'Che'_Guevara).

There are times when guerrillas adopted names from fables. One example of a name that a guerrilla bore that was taken from a folktale is *Chinotomba* (That which pricks or bores). This folktale was common to most people who attended primary school in the late 1960s to the mid-1970s and was taken from the Grade Four (Standard Two) textbook called *Nzwisisai* in a folktale titled 'Kupera kwavanhu' (1970: 22-24). According to the folktale, young boys were herding goats when they discovered a beehive and they wanted to get the honey. They however failed because of the bees that stung them. One day as they were on their usual task, they saw an old man whom they asked to assist them get the honey. The old man did that but he told them not to tell anyone that he, *Chinotomba* had assisted them to get the honey or they would all perish by that which had killed the goats (*munopera nechakapedza mbudzi*). Unfortunately for the boys, they got so satiated that when they got home they were only drinking water, because that is the effect of honey on people – they become so thirsty. One of the parents was worried and suspected that her son had had a meal in other households, a practice that is not encouraged among the Shona. She beat up her son and he confessed that he had eaten honey that had been extracted by *Chinotomba*. Upon confession, they boy dropped dead.

The mother was so shocked by the development that she told the parents of the other boys who were out herding goats with her son. When they were all asked they confessed and also died. One statement they told their parents before they died was that *Chinotomba* had warned them that if they were to ever mention him as the person who extracted the honey and give them, "*Munopera nechakapedza mbudzi*" (You will be finished off by that which wiped out the goats). The name was a warning that people should not be too curious on certain things. If they were, they would face a fate similar to that of goats that were all killed by a leopard because they got attracted by its skin. The parents of the deceased children followed up on *Chinotomba* whom they finally located. *Chinotomba* assisted them and gave them magic roots – one red, one white and another one black. They were to go to a very high mountain where they were to boil each in its own pot. As each pot boiled, they were to shout the words, "*Mvura yako yavira Chinotomba*" (Your water has boiled Chinotomba). When these words were shouted all the children that had died came back to life.

Despite the fact that in Zimbabwe's war of liberation no one was brought back to life after the war, what was here significant was the name *Chinotomba* (That which pricks or bores) and the statement "*Munopera nechakapedza mbudzi*." That which wiped off the goats in the war circumstances are the guerrillas who were fighting for the restoration of their land as well as getting democracy and majority rule entrenched in the country. The ones who would be wiped out by that which wiped off the goats were the whites who were refusing to give the blacks their land back.

It is essential to also note that guerrillas did not take kindly to people who held views that were contrary to theirs. Anyone who was perceived to be different or was found out to be an informer was summarily executed and in most cases his or her relatives were not allowed to bury the deceased. The execution was done publicly as a warning to others to discourage them from doing the same. In this situation, the name *Chinotomba*, and the statement *chakapedza mbudzi* assumed a new meaning that was a warning to the masses not to inform on the guerrillas to the Rhodesian security forces. They were also not to give guerrillas poisoned clothes and food. This means that the masses had to buy the clothes for the guerrillas on their own and not accept donations.

The name *Chinotomba* may also have been a warning to the guerrillas and the masses not to indulge in sexual escapades. During the war of liberation for Zimbabwe, among the guiding principles that were taken from Mao tse Tung's *Red Book* was that guerrillas were not to take liberties with men or women. In short, they were not to commit adultery. While it is true that the sexual act is a tiring one, there was also the fact that if ever there were to be liaisons between the guerrillas and some young women (some who had husbands who had joined the armed struggle), they were not only likely to lose credibility in the eyes of the masses. There were also chances that there would be some men who would have had their wives and daughters who would have been in amorous relations with the guerrillas who would not take kindly to such violations of their family and conjugal relations. The affected parties were likely to take revenge by reporting the guerrillas to the Rhodesian security forces as Sabina's father in *Black Fire!* (Raeburn 1981) had done. So in these circumstances, *chakapedza mbudzi* would be affecting the guerrillas.

Pfukwa and Barnes (2010: 212) point out that guerrilla names are a form of deconstruction where the guerrillas did not only redefine themselves in the new context, but where they as well sought to restructure and reshape or even alter concepts at new levels from which one could look at them differently. This very act of redefining and renaming as well as deconstructing the colonial psychological space that had been erected in the minds of the blacks is captured and summed up in the *nom de guerre Zvichapera* (All this will come to an end). The name was directed at the whites, especially the intransigent Ian Smith and his cabinet who believed that they were fighting communism and defending the Christian civilisation. The guerrillas, some of whom had grown up and learnt the evils of racism were warning the Rhodesians and telling them that it was not beneficial to them and their families to hold on to power because all their rule and power was going to come to an end. In a way, *Zvichapera* was being used as a prophetic name just like God had asked Ahaz to give his children names that were going to make them living symbols of His message to the people of Judah (Isaiah 8: 1-18). The names that Yahweh gave for Ahaz's children are *Shear-jashub* (Isaiah 7: 3 [Only a remnant shall return]) and *Maher-shalal-hash-baz* (Isaiah 8: 1-4 [Pillage hastens, looting speeds]). Like Ahaz's children's names, the name *Zvichapera* was a living symbol of the black's wrath against the white government of Rhodesia. But in addition to that, it was a statement of hope to the blacks that white racial rule was going to end.

The name *Zvichapera* was also intended to give hope to both the guerrillas and the masses. There were some among the guerrillas who had joined ZANLA forces believing that the war of liberation was not going to last long. These ones were being given hope that the war was surely going to end, but they had to endure a lot of suffering, and many battles had to be fought before they finally achieved their objective. To the masses who were making material and human sacrifices, the name was again meant to encourage the masses

144

to continue supporting the guerrillas. The guerrillas also realised that some among the masses had lost their children as well as property and livestock, an in most cases this was due to punitive excursions that the Rhodesians embarked on after they had suffered, at the hands of the guerrillas major strategic and military as set-backs as well as huge casualties in a given area. The name is therefore a form of pre-given and post-given condolences to those who would have suffered.

Gabarinocheka (The tin cuts) is one of the commonest guerrilla names that were used during the war of liberation. There has been a *Gabarinocheka* in almost every area where ZANLA forces operated. This war name is a complex nominal construction that is made up of two components. These are the subject and predicate where *Gaba* is the subject and *rinocheka* is the predicate. As has been discussed in the earlier chapters, when two words or more in Shona are used to form a personal name or any other noun that has special meaning they become one word, hence *Gabarinocheka*.

The name was used to refer to the guerrilla fighters as people who were perceived as insignificant by the Rhodesian authorities and forces. They were seen as a can or tin that had been used and therefore deserved to be thrown away. Through this name, the head of the guerrillas was telling the world at large, and the Rhodesian forces that they were like empty tins that had been emptied everything. While the tin appeared to have had no consequence, just like a used can or tin, the name is a bold declaration that nothing was going to happen to the guerrillas. They were like used tins of beef or beans and anyone who abused them were likely to be seriously injured or were to have cuts on himself. The meaning could also be extended to the masses that on the surface appeared docile and harmless. These as well had the potential to unleash devastating harm on the white Rhodesian community through acts of sabotage such as the digging of roads, the rustling and slaughter of farm cattle as well as the burning down of shops and the filling of dip-tanks with stones as well as the destruction of local government infrastructure such as beer halls and bars. It was also possible that through this name, the bearer of it was informing others guerrillas and the masses that the best mark of a fighter, whether armed or not was to inflict intense harm and destruction, not only on the enemy forces but also on the structures that supported and sustained him, as well as boosted his morale and kept it high.

Shumbayaonda (The lion has grown thin, the lion has lost weight) is the name of another guerrilla who operated at Nyadowa in early to mid-1979. It could not be verified whether this person was the same or related to the late Shumbayaonda Chandengenda of Mashonaland West. As a guerrilla name, the *nom de guerre* possibly meant that blacks were suffering in their own land because they had no economic power. The name may have come from the statement that is normally given by those of the *Shumba* (Lion) totem that *Shumba yofure sora* (The lion has now become a browser), a statement meant to highlight deepening financial or material crises. The name may also have meant that the bearer and his comrades had a huge hungering to spill the blood of the Rhodesian forces. It was only after they had accomplished their mission that they would feel satisfied.

Another possible meaning that this name may have carried could have been a reference to the whites who were in power in Rhodesia. They were in this case the lion that had lost weight due to the incessant guerrilla attacks that had slowed down economic activities in some part of the country and also heightened the pace of migration from the country as more whites escaped from the escalating war that did not appear to have an end in sight.

Conclusion

This chapter has discussed only fifteen names out of a plethora of sentential *noms de guerre* that were borne by some of the guerrillas who fought for the liberation of Zimbabwe in the ranks of the ZANLA forces, the military wing of ZANU. It has focused only on the war names of some of the guerrillas who operated in Nyanga district, in Nyamaropa and Nyadowa, as well as who operated in Katerere as well as in Mutasa district. The researcher has noticed that the guerrillas who embarked on the war of liberation saw themselves as fighting a war that had been left unfinished in the years 1896 and 1897 when both the Shona and Ndebele rose against the white settlers but lost the war. The chapter has as well observed that the fighters adopted *noms de guerre* not only to hide their real identity from the Rhodesian forces, but that the adoption and use of new names was an act of defiance as well as one of redefinition, where each guerrilla saw him or herself as a new being who was going to fight for the liberation of the country. It was also noted in this chapter that since the guerrillas used different names, some of which were sentences, they did this with the intention of relaying messages to the masses, the Rhodesian forces and as forms of address to fellow guerrillas. As statements, some of these sentential names took different forms and had different voices. Some names like *Tafirenyika* encouraged the guerrillas to be brave, so that they would have the courage to face death if it became necessary. There are some names like

Bataihana that discouraged the masses as well as fellow guerrillas from betraying others to the Rhodesian authorities. The chapter has as well observed that some war names were threats that were directed at the Rhodesian forces and other whites who supported Smith that they were fighting in vain because racism was a lost cause in a world that was changing fast. An interesting dimension that was noted about most of the war sentential names was that they have some similarities with some theophoric names in that they take the form of imperative clauses where the masses are at times being compelled to tow the ZANU and ZANLA line. What has come out clearly is that even though the names that were discussed in this chapter are war names, they are very much like the others discussed in chapters 3 and 4 in that they all show that they are products of their immediate environment. They are still very much grounded in the Shona naming practice that dictates that names have to be significant, not meaningless labels. They have to communicate to the wider community.

Chapter VI

Conclusion

This book has discussed and highlighted Shona sentential names as a means that is used by the Shona, specifically the Manyika as a means of relaying messages to different people. It has discussed these names on in three different categories, not because these are enough, but because the researcher is of the opinion that they are representative enough. The study has focused on the Manyika, a group of Shona speakers who are found in both Zimbabwe and Mozambique, hence the names Manicaland (in Zimbabwe) and Manica (in Mozambique). It has however focused on only two districts that are in eastern Zimbabwe that are Mutasa and Nyanga. The bulk of the research focuses on Nyanga. Mutasa only comes into the picture in as far as it housed some guerrillas who overlapped in their operations between the two political districts that may in the war times may have according to ZANLA demarcations fallen into one operational zone. Mutasa also comes into the picture because part of the Tangwena chieftaincy fell under Mutasa in the area that the white settler regime in Rhodesia called Holdenby but which the Tangwena call Mashena (Machena).

One aspect that the book has highlighted is that Shona names are not mere labels that are attached to people, but are words or sets of words by which people are addressed or referred to. It has noted that names among the Manyika and the other Shona groups in general are carriers of messages. They are not innocent. This truth cuts across all names, whether they are of human beings, dogs or cattle. What came out clearly in this research is that in most cases when the Manyika give names, they give 'talking names' that is names that create statements by either making declarations or by giving statements that reflect the namer's ideas or thoughts on a given area or given circumstances. In short, the research has brought to the fore the fact that names are living testimonies of different people's experiences.

The research has also noted that despite the fact that there are numerous books that have been published on Shona names, there is still a lot that has to be done in this area in an effort to give to the world a better insight into the practices of the Shona. This is very important because some historians have labelled the Shona a peace loving people. The question that some of the names raise is, is it not possible to state that the Shona fought their wars not through metal and shields of hides, but in some instances through words? The book is therefore a call to both academics and other interested parties to research further into this area that also carries a lot that relates to Zimbabwe's cultural heritage. It has as well noted that even though names are linguistically placed under parts of speech, and in sociolinguistics are given the name onomastics, they are much more than that because they also function as heritage bearers as well as platforms of cultural expressions. It is clear from the names that have been discussed in this chapter that names are part of cultural practices and expressions as given in the UNESCO 2003 Convention on Intangible Cultural Heritage. When they come up as expressions, names also become part and parcel of social practices in that they may be used to express the namer's opinion on political or religious matters. It is for this very reason that the book has observed and asserted that Shona names then become bolts and nuts of a living heritage.

The book has also observed that while names are cultural expressions and platforms, they also function as a means of communication. As a means of communication, what has come out in the discussion is that names communicate to the world the namer's joys, sorrows or tribulations. They therefore become living summaries and symbols of life's scars and landmarks. They tell the story of the journey that the namer would have travelled. In addition to conveying messages, names also function as memory centres. They play a major role as depositories of the histories of particular periods. This reality comes out very noticeably in the names that are discussed in this book. Besides the names that are given in a socio-economic environment that reflect and tell the history of a people from a social perspective, such as people suffering from the effects of a prolonged drought, some names that are of a religious nature are pointers to the acceptance of Christianity as a guiding faith for some people in the country. Such religious names, especially those that are in the indigenous languages are also pointers not only to the spread and growth of the Christian faith among the Manyika, but are as well indicators of the appropriation and domestication of the Christina faith.

The third category of names that has been discussed is that of war names. The war names are also bearers of history because in them are embedded indicators of the hate and brutality that was part and parcel of the war of liberation. They also tell the now forgotten story by some of the veterans of Zimbabwe's liberation war that it is not only those who had arms that fought the war but also the masses who gave the support as well as the platform for them to successfully re-launch the Second *Chimurenga/Imfazo* war.

Besides being carriers of history, the book has also observed that names are cultural expressions. It has noted that it is not proper to speak ill of how people name their children, because to do that would be going against the letter and spirit of the 2005 Convention on the Protection and Promotion of the Diversity of Cultural Expressions. One thing that the chapter has underscored is the fact that cultural heritage, whether tangible or intangible cannot thrive in an environment that is devoid of tolerance to cultural diversity as well as multiplicity of cultural expressions.

The book has as well observed that it is the entrenchment of values that relate to the appreciation of cultural diversity and expressions that promote and safeguard in addition to preserving cultural heritage. Names, as can be perceived in those that have been discussed in this book, safeguard and preserve as well as promote the naming practices of the Manyika in particular and the other Shona in general. Among these people, names are not just mere attachments but are loaded statements that have to be decoded and appreciated. They are not symbols of a people gone mad, but of a people that are very much anchored in its traditions and has adopted its traditions and some of its practices in a constantly changing environment so that they continuously guide them. The book has argued that to deny people a chance to name themselves is as good as genocide, because when people lose their practices which are part of their identity, they cease to exist as a people. They become live fossils. Such acts can therefore be equated to genocide because foreign naming practices fall into the category of onomastic erasure where names are used to erase a people's identity and memory. This act of onomastic erasure is as good as genocide according to the 1948 United Nations Convention on the Prevention and

Punishment of the Crime of Genocide that in item (b) speaks against acts that cause serious bodily or mental harm to members of a particular group. The Manyika, like the other Shona should therefore not participate in erasing their history as well as destroying their heritage because in doing that, they will be destroying their future and thus themselves.

What this book boils down to is the fact that names, especially Shona ones are very important and they do not have to be taken lightly. They have to be appreciated and promoted.

References

Agyekum, K. 2006. The Sociolinguistic of Akan Personal Names. In *Nordic Journal of African Studies* 15(2) 206–235.

Anderson, 2007. *The Grammar of Names.* Oxford: Oxford University Press.

Asante, M. 2007. *The Historyu of Africa: The Quest for Eternal Harmony.* New York and London: Routledge.

Austin, R. 1975. *Racism and apartheid in southern Africa Rhodesia.* Paris: UNESCO

Beach, D.N. 1980. *The Shona and Zimbabwe, 900-1850.* Gwelo: Mambo Press.

Best, J.W. and Khan, J.V. (1993). *Research in Education*, 7th Ed, London, Boston.

Chakaipa, P. 1961. *Pfumo Reropa.* Salisbury: Longman.

Chalker, S. and Weiner, E. 1994. *Oxford Dictionary of English Grammar.* Oxford and New York: Oxford University Press.

Che Guevara, E. 1961. *Guerrilla Warfare.* New York: Monthly Review Press.

Chitando, E. 2001. Signs and Portents? Theophoric Names in Zimbabwe. In *Word & World Volume XXI, Number 2, Spring* 144-151.

Chivaura, W.B. 1996. Kutya Kurova. In *Nhaka Yenhetembo.* Harare: Longman Zimbabwe. Pp. 33-4.

Chung, F. 2006. *Re-living the Second Chimurenga: Memories from the Liberation Struggle in Zimbabwe.* Harare and Stockholm: Weaver Press and The Nordic Africa Institute.

Cohen, L, Manion, L. and Morrison, K. (2011). *Research Methods in Education.* (7th Ed). London and New York: Routledge.

155

Cummings, L. 2009. *Pragmatics: A Multidisciplinary Perspective.* Edinburgh: Edinburgh University Press.

Denzin, N. (1989). *Interpretive Interactionism.* London: Sage.

Elbourne, P. 2005. *Situations and Individuals.* Cambridge, MA: MIT Press.

Evans, G. 1982. *The Varieties of Reference.* Blackwell, Oxford.

Finnegan, R. 2012. *Oral Literature in Africa.* Cambridge: Open Book Publishers. E-Book.

Fortune, G. 2004. *Essays on Shona Dialects.* Harare: African Languages Research Institute (ALRI).

Gall, M. D. Borg, W. R. and Gall, J. P. (1996). *Educational Research: An Introduction,* New York, Longman.

Geurts, B. 1997. Good News about the Description Theory of Names. *Journal of Semantics, 14.* 319-48.

Haber, H. 2001. Theophoric Names in the Bible. In *Jewish Bible Quarterly 29.* 56-9.

Hargreaves, D.J., Colman, A.M. and W. Slunkin. 1983. The Attractiveness of Names. In *Human Relations, Volume* 36, *Number* 4, 393-402.

Jackson, A.P. 1957. The Names of the vaShona. *Native Affairs Department Annual (NADA) XXXIV.*

Jacobs, J.U. 1995. 'Names for Nomads in The Songlines by Bruce Chatwin' *Nomina Africana* 9(2). 11- 22.

Jones, A. 2011. *Genocide: A Comprehensive Introduction.* (Second Edition). New York: Routledge.

Jordan, P. 2011. Name and Place: Contributions to toponymic literature and research. United Nations Group of Experts on Geographical Names. Working Paper Number 67.

Kadhani, M. and Riddel, R. 1981. Education. In Stoneman, C. (Ed) *Zimbabwe's Inheritance.* London, Basingstoke and Salisbury: Macmillan Press and College Press.

Kahari, G.P. 1990. *The Rise of the Shona Novel: A Study in Development*. Gweru: Mambo Press.

Kahari, G.P. 1986. *Aspects of the Shona Novel and Other Related Genres*. Gweru: Mambo Press.

Key, D. (1997). A community organiser's perspective on citizen participation: Research and the researcher – Practitioner partnerships, *American Journal of Community Psychology*. Washington, D.C.

Kombo, K.K. and Tromp, D.L.A. 2006. *Proposal and Thesis Writing: An Introduction*. Nairobi: Paulines Publications Africa.

Kuimba, G. 1965. *Tambaoga Mwana'ngu*. Salisbury: Longman.

Larson, R. and Segal, G. 1995. Knowledge of Meaning. Cambridge, MA: MIT Press.

Lohman, C.M. and MacPherson, R.I. 1983. Rhodesia: Tactical Victory, Strategic Defeat. *War since 1945 Seminar and Symposium*, Marine Corps Command and Staff College Marine Corps Development and Education Command Quantico, Virginia 22134, 7 June 1983.

Longman Rhodesia. 1970. *Nzwisisai: Shona Series*. Salisbury: Longman.

Maenzanise, B. 2008. The Church and Zimbabwe's Liberation Struggle. In *Methodist History, 46:2 (January)*, 68-86.

Makari, C. *Magamba eChimurenga: Josia Tungamirai*. Gweru: Mambo Press.

Makari, C. 1992. *Zvaida Kushinga*. Gweru: Mambo Press.

Makari, C. 1985. *Zvaida Kushinga* (Schools Edition). Gweru: Mambo Press.

Makondo, L. 2009. An Investigation into Anthroponyms of the Shona Society. Unpublished DLitt et Phil Thesis.

Pretoria: Department of African Languages. University of South Africa.

Mandende, P. 2009. A Study of Tshivenḓa Personal Names. Unpublished DLitt et Phil Thesis. Pretoria: Department of African Languages. University of South Africa.

Mapanje, J and White, L. 1983. *Oral Poetry from Africa.* London: Longman.

Mapara, J. 2010. Liberation War Taboos: Exploiting Indigenous Knowledge Systems as a Survival Strategy. In *Zimbabwe International Journal of Language and Culture.* Volume 1, Number 1. 19-33.

Mapara, J. Nyota, S. and Mutasa, D.E. 2011. *Shona Names as Communication and Description: A case of the Manyika.* Port Louis: VDM Publishers.

Mapara, J. and Nyota, S. Suburban blight: Celebrating memory loss through continued use of colonial names. Paper presented at the 11th Linguistics Association of SADC Universities (LASU) Conference, Lusaka, Mulungushi Village, University of Zambia, 9th-11th May 2011.

Mapara, J. and Thebe, S. The canine bridge: Canonyms as a communicative tool among the Ndebele and the Shona. Paper presented at the 11th Linguistics Association of SADC Universities (LASU) Conference, Lusaka, Mulungushi Village, University of Zambia, 9th-11th May 2011.

Martin, D. and Johnson, P. 1981. *The Struggle for Zimbabwe.* Salisbury: Zimbabwe Publishing House.

Maxwell, D.J. 1993. Local Politics and the War of liberation in North-East Zimbabwe. In *Journal of Southern African Studies.* Volume 19, Number 3. 361-386.

Maxwell, D.J. 1995. Christianity and the War in Eastern Zimbabwe: The Case of Elim Mission. In Bhebe, N. and Ranger, T. (Eds) *Society in Zimbabwe's Liberation War. Volume II.* Harare and London: University of Zimbabwe Publications and James Currey Limited. Pp 58-89.

Mungoshi, C. 1975. *Ndiko Kupindana Kwamazuva.* Gwelo: Mambo Press.

Nyota, S., Mutasa, D.E. and Mapara, J. 2009. Purposeful Naming: A case of beer halls named from colonial Rhodesia to present day Zimbabwe. In *Journal of Social Development in Africa. Volume 24:1.* 141-163.

Payne, J. and Huddleston, R. 2002. Nouns and Noun Phrases", in G. Pullum, and R. Huddleston (Eds). The Cambridge Grammar of the English Language. Cambridge: Cambridge University Press.

Pei, M. 1965. *The Story of Language.* New York and Philadelphia: J.B. Lippincott Company.

Pfukwa, C. 2012. *A Dictionary of Chimurenga War Names.* Harare: Africa Institute for Culture, Dialogue, Peace and Tolerance Studies.

Pfukwa, C. 2008. The martial name in the Zimbabwean conflict (1966–1979). In *Language Matters: Studies in the Languages of Africa* 38:2, 236-252.

Pfukwa, C. 2007. The Function and Significance of War Names in the Zimbabwean Armed Conflict (1966-1979). Unpublished DLitt et Phil Thesis. Pretoria: Department of Linguistics, University of South Africa.

Pfukwa, C. and Barnes, L. 2010. Negotiating identities in guerrilla war names in the Zimbabwean war of liberation. In *African Identities,* Vol. 8, no. 3, 209-219.

Pongweni, A.J.C. 1983. *What's in a Name? A Study of Shona Nomenclature.* Gweru: Mambo Press.

Raeburn, M. 1981. *Black Fire! Accounts of Guerrilla War in Rhodesia*. Gwelo: Mambo Press.

Ranger, T. 1997. Violence Variously Remembered: The Killing of Pieter Oberholzer in July 1964. In *History in Africa, Vol. 24*, 273-286.

Scullard, H.H. *From the Grachii to Nero: A History of Rome from 133 BC to AD 68*. London: Methuen and Company.

Smith, I.D. 2007. *Bitter Harvest: The Great Betrayal and the Dreadful Aftermath*. Johannesburg: Jonathan Ball Publications.

Tungamirai, J. 1995. Recruitment to ZANLA: Building a War Machine. In Bhebe, N. and Ranger, T. (Eds). Soldiers in Zimbabwe's Liberation War. Harare: UZ Publications, pp. 36-47.

Wolcott, (1990). *Qualitative inquiry in Education: The continuing debate, Oklahoma State University Thesis Handbook*. Oklahoma State University.

Zvarevashe, I.M. 1978. *Gonawapotera*. Salisbury: College Press.

Zvarevashe, I.M. 1976. *Kurauone*. Salisbury: College Press.

Zvobgo, C.J. 1986. Aspects of Interaction between Christianity and African Culture in Colonial Zimbabwe, 1893-1934. *Zambezia* (1986), XIII (i), (43-57).

Zvobgo, R. J. 1985. *Transforming Education: The Zimbabwean Experience*. Harare: College Press.

United Nations Documents

United Nations Group of Experts on Geographical Names. Working Paper No. 69 Activities relating to the Working Group on Exonyms (Prepared by Peter Jordan (Austria)), Twenty-sixth session, Item 14 of the provisional agenda. Vienna, 2-6 May 2011.

United Nations Group of Experts on Geographical Names. Working Paper No. 29 rev.1 Geographical names and cultural heritage (Prepared by Hein Raghoebar M.Sc.), Twenty-sixth session, Item 17 of the provisional agenda. Vienna, 2-6 May 2011.

UNESCO 2003 Convention for Safeguarding Intangible Cultural Heritage

UNESCO 2005 CONVENTION on the Protection and Promotion of the Diversity of Cultural Expressions

UNESCO 2001 Universal Declaration on Cultural Diversity

UNESCO 1972 World Heritage Convention

Webliography

Africa Confidential. Runaida Joice Mugari Mujuru (Teurai Ropa (Spill blood')
http://www.africa-confidential.com/whos-who-profile/id/3046 Accessed on 14 February 2013.

All About Religion. History of Christianity in Africa. http://www.allaboutreligion.org/history-of-christianity-in-africa-faq.htm Accessed on 01 February 2013.

Behind the Name: The Etymology and History of First Names. http://www.behindthename.com/name/david Accessed on 13 February 2013.

British Broadcasting Corporation (BBC). The Story of Africa: Christianity. http://www.bbc.co.uk/worldservice/africa/features/storyofafrica/index_section8.shtml Accessed on 14 February 2013.

British Parliament. Rhodesia: Future of Tangwena Children HL Deb 04 August 1972 vol 334 cc614-6 http://hansard.millbanksystems.com/lords/1972/aug/04/rhodesia-future-of-tangwena-children Accessed on 14 February 2013.

Cumming, S. Names. 2012. The Stanford Encyclopedia of Philosophy (Spring Edition), Edward N. Zalta (ed.), URL = http://plato.stanford.edu/archives/spr2012/entries/names/ Accessed on 14 February 2013.

Devitt, M. and Hanley, R. (Eds). 2003. Speech Acts and Pragmatics. Blackwell Guide to the Philosophy of Language. http://userwww.sfsu.edu/kbach/Spch.Prag.htm Accessed on 16 February 2013.

Grundy, T. and Miller, B. 1979. The Farmer at War. Salisbury: Modern Farming Publications www.rhodesia.nl/farmeratwar.html Accessed on 16 February 2013.

Heymann, L.A. 2011. Naming, Identity, and Trademark Law. In the College of William & Mary Law School Scholarship Repository. Faculty Publications. Paper 1122. http://scholarship.law.wm.edu/facpubs/1122 (383-445) Accessed on 17 February 2013.

Internet Encyclopedia of Philosophy. Just War Theory. www.iep.utm.edu/justwar/ Accessed on 17 February 2013.

Malamud. 2007. Lectures on pragmatics: acting with speech http://people.brandeis.edu/~smalamud/ling100/outline12.pdf Accessed on 16 February 2013.

Meharg, S. J. 2006. Identicide: Precursor to Genocide. Working Paper Number 05. Ottawa: Centre for Security and Defence Studies (CSDS).

http://www3.carleton.ca/csds/docs/working_papers/MehargWP05.pdf Accessed on 15 October 2012.

SIL International. 2004. What is a Sentence?
www.sil.org/linguistics/GlossaryOfLinguisticTerms/WhatIsASentence.htm Accessed on 14 February 2013.

Wikiquote. Ian Smith
http://en.wikiquote.org/wiki/Ian_Smith Accessed on 14 February 2013.

Wikiquote. Ernesto 'Che' Guevara.
en.wikiquote.org/wiki/Ernesto_'Che'_Guevara Accessed on 14 February 2013.

Wikipedia, the Free Encyclopedia Descriptivist theory of names
http://en.wikipedia.org/wiki/Descriptivist_theory_of_names 15 December 2012.

Wolska, M. 2007 May. Pragmatics and Discourse Speech Acts or Can You Pass Me the Salt? www.coli.uni-saarland.de/courses/pragmatics-07/Slides/PD.07.3.SpeechActs.pdf Accessed on 14 February 2013.

UNESCO World Heritage Centre. World Heritage.
http://www.whc.unesco.org/en/about Accessed on 14 February 2013.

University of Massachusetts Amherst Campus, Center for Heritage and Society. What is Heritage?
http://www.umass.edu/chs/about/whatisheritage.html Accessed on 14 February 2013.

www.ingramcontent.com/pod-product-compliance
Lightning Source LLC
Chambersburg PA
CBHW022320280326
41932CB00010B/1172

* 9 7 8 9 9 5 6 7 9 0 7 5 3 *